Rebel Baseball

To Jim
Think Baseball

To Jim

Think Baseball

STEVE PERLSTEIN

Rebel Baseball

The Summer
the Game was
Returned
to the Fans

ONION PRESS INC.
Minneapolis, Minnesota

Additional copies of this book may be ordered directly from the
publisher for $22.00 per copy plus $3.00 per copy shipping and
handling. Multiple-copy discounts are available. For more
information or to order, write to:

Direct Sales Department
Onion Press, Inc.
4110 Nicollet Avenue South
Minneapolis, MN 55409-1518

Jacket and interior design by David J. Farr, *ImageSmythe.*
Art by Nancy Wirstig McClure, *Hand-to-Mouse Arts.*

This text is printed on recycled paper using soy-based inks.
Printed in the U.S.A.

Library of Congress Cataloging-in-Publication Data

Perlstein, Steve, 1965–
      Rebel baseball : the summer the game was returned to the fans /
  Steve Perlstein.
      p. cm.
    ISBN 0–9640334–9–6 : $22.00
    1. St. Paul Saints (Baseball team) I. Title.
GV875.S75P47   1994
796.357'64'09776581--dc20   94–8634
                                                                      CIP

To Jennifer. I love you.

FOREWORD

Rarely does life live up to one's expectations. It usually starts out the right way, but somewhere along the line somebody tells us that there isn't a Santa Claus, that we are not going to write the great American novel, or bat .250 in our after-work sandlot league. What makes the human animal so wonderful (and what my friend, Karen, says what makes life a great trip) is our refusal to grasp and deal with reality. None of us involved in the Northern League had a particularly firm grasp of reality. Not Miles Wolff, the primary architect, author, baseball historian, and, most importantly, franchise operator; not Marv Gold-klang, who would rather deal in horseflesh than in commodities (a rare thing indeed for a Yankees fan); and not Bill Murray, whose public life is made up of trying to hide a tremendous depth of feeling. None of us had any right to expect the way things turned out for inaugural flight of the Northern League. Even after all these months and having personally experienced it, I find myself incapable in some ways of describing exactly what happened. It think (and because it's magical, I really don't know), it comes down to two intangibles.

The first was the depth of desire of our players. Cast-offs, wanna-be's, make-believers—in short, players with no grasp of reality. They thought they could still play. Major league organizations felt differently. Forty of those players returned to major league organizational ranks. I guess there's just no predicting that intangible known as desire.

The second element which could not have been predicted was the love affair that sprang up between a team of cast-offs and the folks in the stands. Never was it more painfully evident that we all, when reduced to a common denominator, are and feel the same. People in the stands stood and cheered for players who scratched and clawed—in short, did everything necessary to get another chance. Everybody on the field and in the stands had made mistakes and understood the beauty of a second chance.

St. Paul, for the summer of '93, was like a long, continual party where anything was possible and scale had no bearing on the size of dreams. As you make your way through Mr. Perlstein's very faithful recollection of a magical summer, you will find a cast of characters. Not corporate types but real individuals with big talents and bigger flaws. Whether it was Bull Durham calling home to tell his daughter he hit a home run for her or Bill Murray, arguably one of the most famous faces in the world, trying desperately just to fit in, to be a member of the team. It has taken me three weeks of false starts to attempt to find the words to do justice to a memory that is burned indelible into the back of my brain in a place normally reserved for loved ones, family anecdotes, and "little moments" that are, for whatever reason, unforgettable. When I am old, toothless, and rocking on the porch, I will turn to whomever will listen and say, "You should have seen St. Paul back in '93. It was the greatest summer of my life."

—MIKE VEECK

ACKNOWLEDGMENTS

This book has taken up the better part of the last year and a half of my life—more time than I had allotted for it, and more than I ever dreamed it would swallow up. When a project takes that long and actually comes to fruition, it is only because of the help, support, and encouragement of a host of others. My name is on the front of this book, but here is where I will give credit to those who deserve it so much.

When I first called Northern League president Miles Wolff in August 1992 and said I thought it would be fun to write a book about his new league, he was skeptical and told me I would have to learn much more about minor league baseball before he or anyone else could take me seriously. He was right, and he did take me seriously after I studied and passed his tests, and I am grateful to him for his help. He put me in touch with Mike Veeck, who was as cooperative as he could be from the first day forward, and who ultimately made it possible for me to have such complete access to his team, the essential ingredient in this book. Veeck's partner and boss, Marv Goldklang, always had time for me and my questions. The Saints' staff, starting with general manager Bill Fanning and Media Relations Director Dave Wright, and extending to Annie Huidekoper, Tom Whaley, Pete Orme, Dan Craighead, Stephanie Baumgartner, Al Frechtman, Jessica Jensen, and John Spolyer, made time for me when they had none, and tolerated me when it would have been more expedient to tell me to leave.

Thanks to Linda Cullen for her friendship, and for her photographs.

I am also indebted to the general managers of the other five Northern League teams and their staffs. Gary (The Canary) Weckwerth, Dave True, Doug Stewart, Tom Van Schaack, Kevin Morteson, and their crews made my life much easier during the three months I spent on the road with the Saints. Northern League officials Van Schley, Tom Leip, Nick Belmonte, and David Kemp helped me at many points along the way with background, advice, and some really funny stories that kept me laughing on long days.

This could almost go without saying, but it would be an omission too immeasurable to justify. I asked the players and coaches of the 1993 St. Paul Saints, the team's employees and associates, and many of its fans to let me invade their lives for four months. Most were more than generous with their time, stories, and friendship. Even those who would rather I had not been there that summer were gracious enough to tolerate my presence. To all of them I am truly grateful.

I must also thank so many people outside this small universe who helped in so many ways. My agents, Ling Lucas and Ed Vesneske at Nine Muses and Apollo, were without fail encouraging and supporting, and they were always giving of their time, regardless of whether their efforts would earn them a dime. Bill Bradley at the St. Paul Pioneer Press, Mike Berardino at Baseball America, and Julio Gomez at the Thunder Bay Chronicle-Journal gave me the correspondent assignments that helped support me financially through the baseball season. David Lamb, Joseph Bosco, Jim Kaat, and Stew Thornley offered not only encouragement, but the kind words you see on the dust jacket of this book. I received invaluable advice about the world of publishing from those such as David McNally, Dave Wood, Norton Stillman, Brian Baxter, Charlie Lippincott, and others who I have forgotten to include, and to whom I apologize profusely. Thank you to my brothers, Rick and Ben, for their encouragement, and especially to my sister, Linda, for her invaluable editing assistance.

Of course, there is support and there is support. Jerry and Sandi Perlstein, Harry and Celia Perlstein, Nate and Florence Rudoy, and Jim and Jann Block, showed their faith in me and in this project with their investments, and I forever will be grateful to them for that.

Lastly, I owe a debt that I only hope I can repay. My wife, Jennifer Block, and our children, Julian and Nora, had to cope not only with financial strain during the reporting and writing of this book, but with my prolonged absence as well. Jennifer is my wife, lover, best friend, and business partner, but she virtually had to take on the role of single parent during this summer, and it was not fair. As a husband and father who puts such a tremendous premium on my time with my family, these were separations that caused me immense heartache. I know how difficult this time was for them as well, and I only hope the finished product was worth it.

— STEVE PERLSTEIN
MINNEAPOLIS, MINNESOTA
FEBRUARY 1, 1994

"I see great things in baseball. It's our game—the American game. It will take our people out of doors, fill them with oxygen, give them a larger physical stoicism. Tends to relieve us from being a nervous, dyspeptic set. Repair these losses, and be a blessing to us.
—WALT WHITMAN

"One of the beautiful things about baseball is that every once in a while you come into a situation where you want to, and where you have to, reach down and prove something."
—NOLAN RYAN

INTRODUCTION

The Big Blue Dome

The weather forecast was explicitly, drearily straight-forward. A steady rain, high in the upper fifties. It would not be the kind of weather in which to play baseball, much less to introduce a baseball team to its lot. This was to be the return of outdoor professional baseball to Minnesota, and it might have been nice if the elements could cooperate to produce a decent day. But gloom stared out from the weather page with an ominous cast. Almost everyone was surprised, then, when the new St. Paul Saints showed up at Municipal Stadium on June 3, 1993, for the first day of prac-tice with their gym bags bristling with bats and full of spikes, gloves and jock straps. The sun was out. It was warm. It was a great day for baseball.

In many ways, the young men who took a wrong turn in the runway leading to the clubhouse and got lost (gen-eral manager Bill Fanning gave everyone wrong direc-tions) could understand why this day was so special. In other, very important ways, they had no idea. For these men personally, they were entering a stadium where they were being paid to play baseball. It was the first time for some of them; others had known the joy of receiving a pay-check for playing the game before but, as recently as a week earlier, thought that they would never know that bliss again. All of them were happy knowing they would be handed their monthly check of $700, or $900, or even $1,200. They were happy to live in the cramped, cheap apartments they were able to afford for themselves, to sub-sist on macaroni and cheese mix and all-you-can-eat buffets, and to go without the disposable cash to buy the luxuries others take for granted, such as going to first-run movies or having a nice dinner out. They were being paid these miniscule salaries to do something they could scarcely call work. The next time you hear a millionaire major-leaguer complain that he wants his contract renegotiated, think of these players and know there are still those who play baseball for the love of the game. They get little else.

But these St. Paul Saints could scarcely begin to appreciate what they represented to those who would pay to watch them play. They would understand later on, as they were egged on by the pulsating crowds and mobbed by the 12-year-olds who just last season only cared about getting Kirby Puckett's autograph. They were a rebirth. For the city they played in, for the region, for baseball.

One of the Saints' first season ticket-holders—a group that would prove to be as loyal and devoted as any in sports—sent in a Top 10 list along with his ticket order, with apologies to late night talk show host David Letterman. The team wound up sending copies to the rest of its season-ticket holders:

Top 10 Reasons to Watch the St. Paul Saints

10. Team won't be moving to Dallas anytime soon.
    (The Twin Cities' hockey team, the North Stars, had just migrated south.)
 9. The green stuff in front of you is grass.
 8. At these prices, you can afford to bring your mother-in-law.
 7. Chance to point out constellations between innings.
 6. Self-serve car wash right down the street.
 5. Can sing "Take Me *Out* to the Ballgame" with a clear conscience.
 4. Owners care more about fan interest than compound interest.
 3. No guys in suits asking what a DH is.
 2. You're in the same tax bracket as the players.
 1. Baseball, baseball, baseball.

Stand on the top row of bleachers at Municipal Stadium in St. Paul and look west. If the day is clear, and the air is free of haze, you can see at the base of the Minneapolis skyline a faint white bubble rising like a marshmallow before the roast. That hideous structure is the Hubert H. Humphrey Metrodome, the building that has come to represent sports in Minnesota. It's almost enough to make plenty of baseball fans weep. It's certainly enough to make them defect to the breezy, sun-drenched metal bleachers in St. Paul, the Twin Cities stadium with the big blue dome, where rain means you don't play; where the lack of it means you will watch a baseball game the way it was intended. This was going to be baseball the way it was supposed to be, and the fans were about to take it back for their own.

If that wasn't enough inducement for folks to go out and watch the St. Paul Saints and the Northern League, maybe they could be enticed by what it wasn't. It was not an affiliated minor league. There were no major league parent organizations (contrary to the insertions of some newspaper copy editors throughout the season), nor was this a Single A, Double A or Any-Other-Kind-Of-A-league (as other copy editors would have had us believe). This was an operation slipping under the radar of big-league baseball.

That would mean no commissioner of baseball telling the league, its officials, and its owners what it could and could not do. No farm directors instructing managers which players to put in the lineup when—for the good of the eventual needs of the major-league club, not out of any concern over whether the minor-league club wins or loses. There would be virtually no players plucked out of the lineup one day when the parent organization decided to move them up to the next level—again, without regard to the fans who might have supported these players all season and developed loyalties to them. Running an affiliated minor-league club, Saints chairman Marv Goldklang said, is like operating a movie theater: you sell the popcorn and turn on the projector, but you have practically no say over what movie is shown, and how long it will be in your theater.

The owners of the six Northern League clubs could show whatever flicks they wanted, and yet they were people who knew just how frustrating it was to live in that movie-theater analogy. Goldklang was a minority owner of the New York Yankees and owned part of four other affiliated minor-league clubs. Sioux Falls Canaries owner Harry Stavrenos was president of the San Jose Giants, San Francisco's entry in the California League. Thunder Bay Whiskey Jacks owner Rickey May used to be the general manager of the Durham Bulls (where he worked for owner Miles Wolff, the founder and president of the Northern League). Sioux City Explorers owner Bill Pereira was president of the Boise Hawks of the Northwest League. And Duluth-Superior Dukes owner Bruce Engel had been in cahoots with Donald Trump to form a third major league in 1990, an effort doomed to fail thanks to Major League Baseball's exemption from federal antitrust laws. These were people who got involved with the Northern League because they wanted to have fun owning baseball teams—something they weren't able to do with their affiliated entries, and something that could only bode well for the league's fans.

Under the cement and metal structure that surrounded Muncicpal Stadium's playing field, the St. Paul Saints dressed for the first time in their white polyester pants and black practice jerseys. They donned their black, logo-free caps (the logo would come later, when the team management finally settled on one), and headed into the dugout for their initiation.

Bill Fanning went first. Shouting to be heard above the rumbling freight trains that passed regularly just beyond the left-field wall, the general manager laid out the team's expectations for the players. Little of what he said had to do with baseball. The fans pay your salary, Fanning told them. This team would forever be compared to the Minnesota Twins, and their task was to show they were different by being accessible and by giving the fans an opportunity to meet and talk to baseball players up close. For minor-league baseball in a major-league town, this would be a powerful drawing card. Come out early, stay late, sign autographs, make personal appearances, talk to the kids, talk to the adults, just be nice. This was mostly a nice bunch of guys, and ones who had not yet been jaded by signing too many autographs, or by making too much money, so they would have no trouble following these instructions. But these qualities were important enough to the success of the St. Paul Saints that Fanning felt compelled to relate them nonetheless.

As he spoke, the players sat on the dugout bench. Actually, dugout isn't quite the right word. Nothing was dug out; the stainless steel bench and its cement casing were at field level. The field had been used for all its years as a high school and college ballpark, and since parents didn't want their kids to be pelted with foul balls. Since the City of St. Paul did not want to pay for the resulting lawsuits, the dugout was shielded by the mesh of a chain-link fence from top to bottom, opening only at the far end to allow players to get in and out. Fanning stood on the other side, separated by the diamond-shaped pattern of metal. As he spoke, train after long, noisy freight train rumbled past, competing with the general manager for the players' hearing capacity, and sometimes winning.

Manager Tim Blackwell went next. He knew few of these men, and most of them didn't know him, or each other. Blackwell, whose trademark mustache had not seen a trimming scissors in four years and inched down past his lower lip, and whose straight brown hair was (for now) free of gray, spread his hands out in front, palms up, for the first of thousands of times this season. "For whatever reason, we're still in this thing. We can all compare release slips and stuff, but we're going to do it just like you do it in elementary school, since nobody knows anybody, we're going to go down the line and have everybody introduce themselves, and you can show off how many times you've been released. I'll start myself. Tim Blackwell, this is year number twenty-four in professional baseball, and I've got three pink slips and I've been fired two other times. And I'm still kicking, and I'm still fighting, and I think there's a lot of fight left. They're going to have to tear this stuff off of me, or bury me in it. I can't help it. I enjoy being out here. I love doing it, and I'll make myself available down the line to any and everybody for as much time as you want."

"My name is Jim Eppard, and I'm the player-coach. I'll be involved with the hitters. I've been released twice and I hope I never get fired, but I'm sure I will. I played for the Angels one time, and the Blue Jays. You don't have to fire me already, do you? I don't have a whole lot to say, but I'm sure we'll get a chance to talk with the hitters and to go over some things and to try to work with you."

"My name is Dave Fricke. I worked with Tim with the Mets. This is my fourth ... no, fifth year in baseball, and I'm here to help you guys, so if you need anything come see me. I've never been released. I resigned last year from the Mets on my own to return to school."

"Greg D'Alexander. I played with the Miracle for two years, and I got released from the White Sox last year."

"Frank Charles. I used to play for the Giants for two years, and I was just released once. Hopefully that's it."

"Eddie Ortega. I was released by the Phillies and the Expos."

"I'm Jerry DeFabbia, I'm from Fairleigh Dickinson University, and I haven't been released yet."

"My name's Eric Moran, and I'm a rookie pitcher."

"Kent Blasingame. Rookie. I played at Texas Tech."

"Rick Hirtensteiner. I've been released twice in the U.S. and once in Mexico."

"My name is Tommy Raffo. I was with the Miracle for one year, with the Reds for two years, and I was just released from the Reds."

"My name is Keith Gogos. I've been booted out of Montreal and booted out of the Angels. So that's oh-for-two."

"John Thoden. I was with the Expos for three years and got released a year and a half ago."

"Scott Meadows. Used to play for Baltimore and just got released this spring."

"Ranbir Grewal. I was with the Expos for three years and just got released."

"Adam Schmlofer. With the Cubs, just released."

"Tony Long. Played with the Royals for three years. Just got released."

"Ed Stryker. I was with the Dodgers for three years and just got released this week."

"Michael Mimbs. I was with the Dodgers for three years and got released in spring training."

"Jim Manfred. I'm from Minneapolis. That's it. I've never played baseball before. Never been released."

The only truthful parts of Manfred's little monologue were his name and the fact that he's from Minneapolis. Really, he'd been cut from baseball teams in high school, college and the pros. Everybody laughed, but it was only a little funny. These players had decided to dedicate their adult lives to this point to a game, a pursuit where maybe one out of every thousand who take it up will reach the pinnacle of the Major Leagues, a vocation and an avocation that absorbs one's life so completely that he has trouble separating everything else out and leading a normal existence. Some had been working only a few years towards that goal, some for a dozen. Sholoffer and DeLong would not be there when the season started in two weeks. Others would arrive later to fill out the twenty-two-man roster. A precious few would make it to the major leagues, and the others would have to make their way for the rest of their lives by a more traditional route, by getting up every morning and going to work behind a desk, or on a factory line, remembering what was, and knowing they at least made the effort. If a ballplayer was in the Northern League, this was the last chance at the brass ring. If success did not come this time, it would not come at all, and everyone knew it. A month and a half earlier, at his press conference announcing his hiring, Blackwell called the Northern League "a second-chance league," for him and for everybody else. Blackwell might as well have said it was a last-chance league, but he was in a charitable mood that day.

Mike Veeck, the president and one-third owner of the Saints, was the last to speak before the ballplaying began.

"This is going to be a terrific thing. The most important thing is it's the start of the baseball season, and that's number one, even though once in a while they'll accuse us of some cheap theatrics—of which we'll be guilty—to get people into the stands. But the number one thing is baseball. This is an adventure. It's a wonderful concept, a new league, and we've really got a chance to shine. There will be a lot of interest and a lot of emphasis on what is happening, so look at it that way. We'll all take the adventure together. And the sun's out, so let's play two. Thanks a lot, you guys. Let's go."

CHAPTER ONE

Play Ball, Already

By the time June 15 arrived, the St. Paul Saints had had enough of practice. They wanted nothing more to do with infield drills, dead-ball batting practice in the cage, intrasquad games, and getting to the field at half past nine in the morning. They were ready to play a real game. If only the bus driver could find the Duluth stadium.

Duluth is an odd little city, barely more than a mile wide and 15 miles long, hugging the western shore of Lake Superior. The city is enduringly linked to the giant lake, from its port, where it derives so many jobs and so much of its economy, to its weather, which can turn from calm and pleasant to positively frigid with one puff of wind off Superior's chilly waters. As it rises from the lake, the City of Duluth keeps on rising, with steep hills that make it look like San Francisco would, if San Francisco had only 100,000 people and not all that much to do past 10 o'clock at night.

Grundy the bus driver (his name tag really said "Grundy"), an old, tediously methodical man with a friendly manner, a round, puffy face with a protruding lower lip—like a caricature, with an oversized head and a tiny body—stood up at the front of the bus after the Saints players and coaches had piled on and addressed the team: "OK, so who knows how to get to the ballpark?"

You could almost hear shoulders drooping and eyebrows raising as these people from Georgia and Cuba and Australia and Arizona looked at each other and wondered if they'd have opening day after all. But Doug McLeod, the team's radio announcer and the one person on that bus who'd actually been to Duluth, saved the day. He knew the general direction Grundy had to drive to get to the park, and a clue gleaned from that day's *Duluth News-Tribune*— advice on the best places to park when attending the game—led the bus to the right neighborhood. Team lookouts spotted lighting standards, and Grundy finally zeroed in on the spot. But he zipped right past the entrance marked "Players and Park Officials Only" and proceeded around the front of the park, around a corner and past the outfield wall into a muddy morass and a dead end. If Grundy was good at anything, though, it was backing up, and he did it well enough that the team could make the walk to the dressing room and begin preparing for a baseball game.

Wade Stadium in Duluth was almost Wade Pile of Rubble in 1986, when the forces of progress wanted to tear it down to put up some structure that would make money for some developers—nobody remembers anymore just what that was. But the park's rich tradition—it hosted the old Duluth-Superior Dukes of the original Northern League on and off for forty years until the circuit fizzled and popped in the early 1970s—and the faint hope that it might one day again host a professional ballclub won the argument, and a group of impassioned civic boosters managed to save the stadium—but not to renovate it.

Until the Northern League showed interest in Wade Stadium, it was a holy mess, an impressive brick facade hiding a sinkhole where teams could still play ball, if they didn't mind a pockmarked field with decrepit stands and almost uninhabitable clubhouses. But the promise of a little baseball can be a powerful motivation, and Wade was now a gleaming, if cramped, edifice, with a 12-foot-high cement outfield wall covered top to bottom and foul pole to foul pole with billboards, a fresh coat of paint leading to the refurbished concession stands, brand-new plastic bleacher seats to put an end to Wade's famous splinters, and new lights in the towers, so players could at least see at night, even if they still couldn't see well.

It was the dugouts that were a problem. The clubhouse steps led down into a dank concrete shaft that usually held plenty of standing water in which mosquitoes could breed; this dungeon fed into three steep steps with a ceiling only five feet above the top one. That was the first time the players had to duck. Even when the stadium maintenance workers staple-gunned a powder-blue shag carpet remnant on the doorway, it was still a dangerous spot; it might not draw blood anymore, but it could induce a thundering headache just the same. The dugout itself was tiny, without enough bench space for even the starting lineup, let alone the entire team, which resulted in Saints and Dukes spilling out across the warning track because they couldn't fit anywhere else. Getting out of the dugout the players had to duck again. The upwardly slanted roof—which, incredibly, was new—extended all the way over the dugout pit and was barely four feet above the last of the three steps, which were so high that players sitting on the bench couldn't see the playing field. People wondered when, not if, someone was going to clock his head on the roof and tumble hair-first to the dugout floor.

The baseball fans of Duluth were not very concerned about the condition of the dugout steps, though. They'd waited twenty-two years for professional baseball to come back to town, and they weren't going to let it go without a fight. Before the gates opened at Wade on opening night, more than three hours before game time, more than 500 people had queued up outside the stadium waiting for their chance to get in. Every parking lot within a mile was filled, and a sea of black and white Dukes paraphernalia converged on the red brick structure. The Dukes' trademark was black tie and tails—like the Duke of Earl—and general manager Tom Van Schaack and his staff were scurrying around the stadium in that garb, looking like they should be at opening night of the opera, not of a baseball game. Van Schaack kept knocking off his top hat with his walkie talkie antenna.

○ ○ ○

This was not the first Duluth Dukes team of a Northern League to play in Wade Stadium. Don Gilmore was a nineteen-year-old pitcher in 1948, during the Dukes' first incarnation. He had just broken in with the Dukes, a Cardinals farm club, and he could throw, with a good fastball and a nasty curve. If he remained healthy and kept developing, this kid from Ohio had a near-certain future as a big-league ballplayer.

That was before the Dukes' team bus was heading south on Highway 36 through the Twin Cities, on the way to another town during a road trip. It was before the steering failed on the truck in the oncoming lane, before the truck rammed into the bus, leaving a wrenched, haunting pile of metal filled with dead and wounded ballplayers. Four players and the team's manager were killed. All but three of the 18 players were seriously injured. Gilmore's wounds sound so gruesome hearing them described 45 years later that it makes it almost impossible to imagine having to live through them. He suffered the excruciating pain of third-degree burns. His right foot was torn off at the ankle. His back was broken. His left thigh was crushed. He will forever be missing a small piece of his skull, taken off by a projectile of flying sheet metal. He broke seven ribs. Gilmore did not learn until two years later that he had cracked his fibia and broken his knee, and he did not find out about the steel plate in his head until three weeks after the wreck. Doctors did not want to upset him further with the news about losing part of his skull, and they had too much else to worry about to even find the broken bones in his leg, though the pain would not have been any better or worse had he known right away. After months in a St. Paul hospital, with his wedding postponed, Gilmore returned home to Columbus—in the train's baggage car, since he could not move well enough to make it to a seat in a passenger car.

Finally, the next year he was married. The couple honeymooned in Duluth.

It was the beginning of a magnetic attraction that kept Gilmore coming back to this city, despite all the pain that comes with the memories it brings. He came back again and again, including for a thirty-year reunion of his ill-fated team in 1978, a visit that included a day of golfing and dining with Bob Hope, who was in Minnesota and had read Gilmore's story in the newspaper, and who was impressed enough to invite him out for the day. Gilmore kept coming back to Duluth during the course of a remarkable life, one that saw him pick up the pieces of his broken bones and shattered psyche and begin an eighteen-year career as a decorated police officer, followed by six terms in the Ohio legislature, which ran concurrently with a career operating a successful security company, after which he founded a company that develops new recycling technologies. "Either you get up and go, or you die," Gilmore would say much later. "I don't know anyone at that age who wants to die."

But he never watched baseball.

After he recuperated from the crash, Gilmore gathered his courage in a tight ball and stepped on a semipro diamond, but he collapsed running to first base in his opening game. He tried coaching during one spring training, but he couldn't take being so close to the field and not playing. He asked his wife, Jean, to take the sports pages out of the paper before she gave it to him in the morning.

But on June 15, 1993, almost forty-five years to the day after a runaway truck bid a jolting farewell to a promising baseball career, sixty-four-year-old Don Gilmore was at Wade Stadium, a dozen rows behind home plate, a spectator at his first full baseball game since that deadly night on Highway 36. You could tell, watching Don Gilmore gaze out at the field where he was to begin his journey to the top, that he was a happy man to be at a ball game again in Wade Stadium. He would tell you as much. Yet tears still welled up in his eyes as he talked about the potential that was lost in a hail of metal shards and broken glass. "There is lots of joy, but there is a lot of sadness, too. I look out there and I see guys that aren't there. I remember how they looked out there when we played ball out here."

The original Northern League and Duluth Dukes continued until the circuit wheezed to a halt in 1971, but it went on without Don Gilmore.

When he heard, almost by accident, that the Dukes and the Northern League were being revived, the homing device in Gilmore's brain kicked in and drew him to the west shore of Lake Superior. "There was no doubt in the world I would be here. My wife said, 'Are you sure you want to go?' I said, 'No.' She said, 'Why are you going?' I said, 'I just have to.'

"On my ball club, everyone had potential. There was no one on the way down. Everyone was on the way up. Even after all these years, I still wonder what would have been. It's just something you never get over. We all still get nightmares. I get four or five a month. It'll take your mind off your golf game, I'll guarantee you."

"C'mon, man, let's get going. I'm getting anxious. I haven't had an opening day in two years."

Leon "Bull" Durham, the St. Paul Saints' main attraction and biggest player (both in myth and physical stature), was swinging his bat in the dugout, nearly knocking loose a couple of heads, waiting for the interminable opening ceremonies to end and the ballgame to begin. Finally, the players were introduced so they could take their places along the baselines for the national anthem.

One by one the announcer called the Saints, but he forgot Stephane Dionne, French Canada's contribution to baseball. Dionne, a catcher, wanted to play baseball so badly that he attended four of the Northern League's six tryouts, sleeping in his car in Florida so he could afford his attempt to latch onto a pro team. Finally, Saints manager Tim Blackwell, himself a catcher, could take no more. He signed Dionne as a bullpen catcher—the lowest position in a league many were wondering if they should even take seriously. But Stephane got to wear a uniform and was paid $500 a month for the privilege, and he did not dream of complaining. But when the announcer skipped over his name, Durham and Blackwell did complain. They did not take well the snubbing of their teammate.

"Come on, Stephane, you come out with me," Blackwell told him as he ran to take his position near home plate.

"You can be assistant manager for a day." Bull l
ward towards the press box and let loose in l
French-accented baritone boom: "Ste*phane!* What about
Ste*phane?* Damn, man!" On the way back to the dugout,
Durham put his arm around the round-faced catcher and
reassured him, "We'll make sure they don't do that to you at
home, man."

Finally, then, after more than a year of preparation,
weeks of practice, hours of nervous anticipation and about
a dozen pregame speeches, the St. Paul Saints were ready to
play the Duluth-Superior Dukes. The visiting Saints began
inauspiciously, going down one-two-three in their half of
the first. But starter Ranbir Grewal had his chance to show
what he and his team could do as he stared down Dana
Williams, Duluth's closest thing to a superstar, who'd had a
couple of cups of coffee, maybe even an entire continental
breakfast, in the big leagues.

With the first pitch, Ranbir plunked him square in the
shoulder.

Things were not going well early on for Ranbir, an imposing pitcher of Indian ancestry, with a goatee and a massive family grape farm to retire to in California if this baseball thing didn't work out. In baseball, pitchers want to
keep the ball low, where it will curve and dart more accu-
rately, and where it is more difficult for hitters to rear back
and hit it as far as they can. Grewal was absolutely not doing
that in the first inning, with his pitches high and very often
outside. He loaded the bases before Eddie Ortega, the
flashy, wiry Cuban second baseman, rescued him by starting a double play to end the inning.

On went the game. And on. And on some more. One
of the Northern League's proudest innovations was the
twenty-second clock, a timer that was to hang in center
field, much like the twenty-four-second clock that rules a
basketball game. Once the pitcher got the ball from the
catcher, he had twenty seconds to throw a pitch. If he did-
n't, the umpire called a ball. If the batter stalled twenty seconds, it was a strike. It was a great idea. All Duluth had to do
was to figure out how to work its clock, which hung on a

center field light standard like a TV without a picture tube. Without a functioning clock, the Saints and the Dukes rambled to a 3-3 tie after nine innings in just over three hours— a long time even for organized baseball, which makes little effort to speed up its games.

For the tenth inning, Duluth manager Mal Fichman put in pitcher Mike Brady, a left hander who threw slow. Painfully slow. Brady is the kind of pitcher that sends hitters running to the batter's box, so excited are they to have the luxury of time as they study the ball ambling its way to home plate. Michael Mimbs, the Saints' starter the next day, looked up and recognized Brady. "Hey, I played with him in the Dodgers organization. He throws nothing but curve balls." Jim Eppard, the team's first baseman and hitting coach, couldn't understand why Mimbs was talking almost to himself. Eppard opened his eyes wide and said almost in disbelief as Jerry DeFabbia began his walk to the plate, "Well, tell Jerry! Tell Jerry!"

Actually, it didn't matter what he told Jerry, because Brady put the first pitch in the small of Jerry's back and DeFabbia trotted to first base. Ortega singled, and Fichman, the Duluth manager, decided to walk Eppard—a player with a reputation around baseball of being able to make contact with the ball at any time and drive in a run when he needs to, and with five minor-league batting titles to prove it—to pitch to Durham.

Then Mal Fichman showed the world and 4,518 Duluthians why he is known around baseball as Mal Function. All night, Bull had been so far in front of pitches that he could swing at strike three, get back to the dugout, and head into the clubhouse for a smoke before the ball reached the catcher. Durham had spent more than a decade in the major leagues, terrorizing pitchers who threw their fastballs at more than ninety miles an hour, a speed most Northern League pitchers simply could not match. Under Wade Stadium's dim lighting conditions—the front office might have been better off running to the hardware store and buying a case of hundred-watt GE bulbs and screwing them in the lighting fixtures—it made Durham look more like an overweight, old ballplayer waving at bad pitches (which he was) than the man who was once one of the most feared power hitters in baseball (which he also was).

That's why no one could figure out why after Fichman walked singles hitter Jim Eppard he took out Brady, who was throwing curveball after looping curveball in the low seventies, and put in Wayne Rosenthal, a former big-leaguer who throws the kind of hard fastballs that Bull dreams about when he's snoring loudly and sleeping with the TV on. But Fichman did, and Rosenthal put two straight fastballs right down Broadway for strikes one and two. Everybody in northeastern Minnesota knew Rosenthal would be coming with more heat, including Bull. Rosey laid the ball over the center of the plate, right about at Durham's belt level. Bull turned on the pitch and sent it towering into the air, where it caught Duluth's stiff lake breeze. The wind carried the shot over the right field fence and into the murky swamp beyond.

Bull Durham. Grand slam. Tenth inning. Opening night.

And Leon, all 230 pounds of him, leaped down the dugout steps, ducked his head and ran into the clubhouse. He lit a cigarette and called his daughter. "That's right, sweetheart, just like you said. I hit a home run."

This is not where Leon Durham was supposed to be as he approached his thirty-sixth birthday. He wanted more. He and plenty of others thought he deserved more.

In Leon Durham's boyhood, baseball was his ideal. As the seventh of ten children in a happy, comfortable, and crowded Cincinnati home, fighting for attention took too much energy. But that house was right down the street from Crosley Field, where the Cincinnati Reds played before they retreated behind the imposing genericness that is Riverfront Stadium. To earn pocket money, Leon would direct Reds fans to his front lawn, where they could tear up his mom's grass for two bucks a car. When he wasn't making money off the Reds, he was living vicariously through them.

He found the modern version of a knothole, an aperture in the concrete stadium wall where a growing boy could watch heroes like Lee May, Pete Rose, and Tony Perez, the legends of the Big Red Machine. It was the kind of boyhood that would happen in a movie if someone wanted to romanticize the life of a young black kid growing up dreaming of being a ballplayer. Everything was going right.

When Durham reached high school, the good fortune continued. He starred in football, basketball, and baseball, a six-foot-two young man with enough strength to power a ball over the right field fence or post up underneath the basket against the toughest opponent. For his senior year, Durham decided to concentrate on baseball, but he also wanted to get a job to earn some pocket money. Prom was coming up, dating was a priority, and Leon wanted to be able to participate in the fun. No problem, his older brothers told him. We'll take care of your pocket money, but you concentrate on sports, on working out and building your strength. They saw their kid brother had a future in baseball, and as his surrogate fathers they were determined that nothing would stand in his way.

As high school graduation and the June amateur baseball draft approached in 1976, the Durhams waited by the phone. It rang early. The St. Louis Cardinals picked Leon in the first round and gave him a $96,000 signing bonus— "a lot of money back then," he remembered. The Cards sent Durham to their rookie-league team in Sarasota, Florida, his first time away from home, away from the family that always supported him and always was there for him when he turned around to look for help. With his safety net gone, Leon felt lost, his mind half on the game and half on Cincinnati. The distraction showed in his statistics. It was a summer of many firsts for Leon Durham: The first time cut from his umbilical cord to his family, the first time he didn't start every game and play every inning, the first time he did not dominate whatever level of baseball he was at. It was scary and confusing. "I couldn't relate to being away from home," he would remember later. "But it was on after that."

That was the kind of scrappy attitude that would mark the rest of his career, and mark the turning point from a teenager with rippling muscles and tremendous potential to a ballplayer who would meet that potential, partly because he convinced himself that he would, and that anybody who tried to take it away from him would do so at his peril. From Sarasota, Durham moved on in the next few years to Cardinals farm clubs in Gastonia, North Carolina; St. Petersburg, Florida; Little Rock, Arkansas; and Springfield, Illinois. That last stop was in 1980, when he was finally called to The Show. "I called Moms. She started crying." In his first big league game, Leon had an RBI triple. It was indeed on.

With the big-league club, "It was great. I never had to go into my pocket for anything. Garry Templeton, Tony Scott, George Hendrick, those guys looked out for me. We made, like, sixty-five dollars a day in meal money, and that just stayed in my pocket. Those guys would see me in the hotel and say, 'Where are you going?' I'd tell them I was going out to eat, and they'd say, 'Wait, we're going with you.' I just sent that money to Moms. She's said that if I never got back to the big leagues, she'd be happy for the life I've been able to give her."

It was a great life for Leon, too. But he let it get too good. In 1983, in the midst of his three straight All-Star Game appearances, when he was ripping twenty home runs a year and hitting around .300, with plenty of money in his pocket, and some new friends who provided the encouragement and the supplies, Durham discovered cocaine. The story is the same for all kinds of athletes, actors, businesspeople, average guys on the street. Coke does not discriminate, nor is there any socioeconomic test required to become a drug addict. It took Durham a while to realize what had happened to him, and a while longer to learn the necessity of leaving that in his past. "I got mixed up with the wrong guys," he would say years later, after he learned to take responsibility for himself, and almost before it was too late to salvage his career. "That was my choice right there. I don't know why it happened, but I thought I could control it. Of course I couldn't. I do regret it, but I'm still alive, I'm sober, and that's what counts." He knows that now, but four years after his first suspension for drugs, he tested positive for cocaine again. He was suffering back problems, he was at the tail end of a three-year, $3.5 million contract (it should have been for two years and $3.5 million more, and Durham was part of the Collusion I and II settlements as a result), and, as he put it with his characteristic rumbling belly laugh, "I was doing things I shouldn't have been doing. But it won't happen again. I'm a fucked up person anyway, why would I need drugs? Now I know what people talk about when they talk about a natural high."

After a decade of major-league baseball with the Cardinals and Chicago Cubs, Leon Durham was a shunned man. With the money from his playing days well-invested, and with a successful printing franchise in Cincinnati, the Durham family could afford to live well. But Leon still felt he had something to prove. He was ready to play again.

If Durham's attitude had improved along with his understanding of his life and his responsibilities, it apparently was still not enough to convince major-league clubs. While pitcher Steve Howe was on his eighth chance to bounce back from cocaine relapses, Leon could not seem to get a third opportunity. He was in spring training with the Chicago White Sox, and he had a good camp. But the choice was between Durham and Bo Jackson, and the Sox decided to pick up their option on Jackson, who was recovering from a risky hip replacement but who was still one of the most bankable stars in sports. They offered Leon a chance at Triple A Nashville, but with no guarantee that he would play regularly. Not good enough.

That's when the St. Paul Saints called. That's when Durham decided to take a chance on an untested league (though he was tested—twice a week for drugs, at the expense of Major League Baseball), a chance to play ball and be the big fish in a small and uncertain pond.

CHAPTER TWO

Home Cooking

The rain began to fall on the morning of June 18—
a murky, dingy sort of drizzle, the kind that annoys you
more than it makes you wet. As evening approached, the
temperature dipped close to sixty, with a sincere promise to
keep on falling. It was not the sort of weather one might
choose for a seminal baseball event, but the St. Paul Saints
front office was enjoying the irony immensely.

When the Saints began to take form nearly a year earlier, Miles Wolff, Mike Veeck, Marv Goldklang and the rest
of the people who formed the vision didn't think of the
team as the return of outdoor baseball to the Twin Cities.
Mike Veeck likes to say he never heard of the term "outdoor
baseball" before, because in his experience it was redun-
dant, a poor economy of words. (Like virtually anything
else Mike Veeck says, it was a statement loaded with a
healthy dose of hyperbole. He usually happens to say that
kind of stuff when there's a microphone in his face.) As
time went on, though, they quickly realized the truth: A
healthy chunk of the tickets they would sell this season and
in the years to come would be bought by people who genuinely missed the chance to watch a ballgame with a breeze
blowing the froth off their beer, with a wind to either knock
down a fly ball or to carry it over the fence. Since 1981 that
had been missing in the Twin Cities. Baseball there had
taken a new form, an antiseptic tinge that comes with an in-
flated Teflon dome and plastic grass. The Hubert H.
Humphrey Metrodome was an unacceptable adulteration
of baseball for tens of thousands of fans in Minnesota.

Baseball in the Dome was like watching the game in an operating theater: sterile and impersonal. The Saints figured out in short order that playing baseball outdoors was a marketing tool they could use to their advantage.

So coping with the elements to get in nine innings was a public relations boon too sumptuous to pass up. So was the ticket and concession revenue from a sellout crowd who ate up $14 T-shirts and $25 sweatshirts and $20 caps almost as quickly as they did hot dogs and peanuts. Unless the players in the field were in imminent danger of drowning, the Saints' brass decided, this game would be played. It came as a surprise to the thousands who called the Saints' office that afternoon of June 18, 1993. ("Municipal Stadium, home of the Saints . . . Unless there's a downpour, we're going to play" is a sequence of words forever burned into the memories of anybody who spent time near a Saints phone that day, or the many damp days that followed.) Chairman Goldklang, president Veeck, general manager Bill Fanning and the rest figured (correctly, it turned out) that everyone would show up in spite of the weather, and that all the local TV stations there with their live units and all the newspapers there with their columnists and photographers would make a big deal out of the fact that Twin Citians could again worry about the weather when they attended a baseball game. A news crew from Channel Nine orchestrated a scene in one of the bleacher sections—when the reporter doing the live shot pointed upward and the camera operator swung his lens towards the stands, everybody opened their umbrellas on cue in a ballet of soggy baseball heritage for the viewers at home. The crowd performed perfectly, and the TV crew had its shot.

Municipal Stadium was a relatively new structure of concrete and steel, little more than a decade old, that suffered slightly from a lack of character the likes of which Duluth had, with its brick facade and old stadium feel—but that more than made up for it by being a refined ballpark in nearly every way, from the neatly paved parking lot to the metal bleachers that made butt slivers an unpleasant memory of the Twin Cities' proud minor-league past. Just past the turnstiles fans were greeted by a too-small concession stand to the left and a table laden with T-shirts, sweatshirts, caps, and seat cushions to the right. On either side of the concession stand, wide ramps led to the three thousand reserved seats, stretching twenty-five rows deep from one dugout to the other, and that were raised ten feet above field level. Beyond that, fans who bought general-admission tickets had to troop down a flight of clanging metal stairs to the stainless steel bleachers that ran the length of each foul line. When the Saints front office had sold every ticket they had and had mashed everyone they could fit into the park, the stadium was teeming with a full house of 5,069 people. Nobody had even a clue at that point just how many times that attendance figure would appear at the bottom of St. Paul box scores. A home run had to travel 320 feet to each foul pole, and 400 feet to dead center. The outfield wall was a sea of freshly painted advertisements for everything from beds to banks to bagels. A brand new scoreboard rose from behind the left-center-field fence. In right center was the twenty-second clock, the Northern League's failed effort at speeding up games. In the few parks where the clocks even worked, the umpires usually forgot to look at them. When they remembered, they didn't know what call to make. By the season's third week, the league had suspended use of the clock indefinitely.

If the structure itself was not particularly distinctive, Municipal Stadium's St. Paul surroundings made up the difference. Just beyond the left-field fence, and across Energy Park Drive parallel to the first base line, were train tracks heading to and from the expansive switching yards of this blue-collar city. Every inning or two, a string of Burlington Northern or Soo Line diesel locomotives would pull a long line of boxcars, hopper cars, and tank cars in one direction or the other past the park. It was almost enough to make one wonder about all the claims that the railroad industry was dying; if all these cars were full, there appeared to be plenty of train business just within sight of the Northern League alone. If the Saints were at bat when a train passed by, the crowd would begin a booming chant of, "Hit the train! Hit the train!" If the engineer blew the horn and waved, he was cheered. And surely he could hear the chorus of boos from 450 feet away if he did not. Over the right-field wall was an eight-story cement block structure with no glass in the windows and black singes around the edges of the openings. Next to it was another concrete building, this one low and long, which also appeared to have been a victim of a few too many kids playing with matches, and it was beside a railroad tank car sitting on a 40-foot stretch of track, never to haul another load of fuel. This was the Twin Cities' firefighter training facility, within a thundering home run to right field of the Saints' home games. Occasionally during those games, crews from one fire department or another would be scaling ladders and climbing fire escapes, practicing their hazardous jobs and providing a little extra entertainment for the price of a baseball ticket.

There's something refreshing, almost cleansing, about watching a baseball game in a setting like this—a fact especially true for baseball fans in the Twin Cities. These are people used to paying five bucks for parking, another twelve for their ticket, three bucks for a program (that's not including the pencil to score with—those cost extra, if you can believe it), three more for a hot dog, and four bucks for a beer, all for the privilege of going inside, where management has precisely measured the proper amount of sunlight allowed to filter through the Metrodome's fabric roof, where great pain has been taken to make the artificial turf look as much as possible like real grass (right down to phony lawn mower tracks), where the big Jumbotron scoreboard will thoughtfully help you choose which bank to go to, which newspaper to read and which beer to drink, all in vivid color with splashy jingles to help you make your decision—it will even tell you when to cheer and what to yell. Every year, millions cheerfully wade into the pit of corporate baseball, at the Metrodome and elsewhere, but it's just not that much fun.

○ ○ ○

The Saints won that home opener against the Thunder Bay Whiskey Jacks, when Scott Meadows rapped a bases-loaded single in the bottom of the ninth for a 2-1 win. Classic. They took the next two against Thunder Bay as well. Was that incidental? Almost. It didn't hurt anything or anybody (except maybe the Whiskey Jacks and the Dukes) that St. Paul ended its first week 5-0 en route to a 6-0 start, or that they gave up a grand total of three runs during that three-game Thunder Bay series and scored twenty during the first two games in Duluth. The baseball was good—better, even, than the hopes of the league's dreamers when they tried to convince people that major-league organizations do indeed make mistakes and those mistakes would form the spine of this league, and much better than the grumbling of those major-league executives who made the mistakes, afraid the world would learn that they were not perfect. A humbling thought, but, as any Northern Leaguer knew all too well, baseball is a humbling game.

During opening weekend, there was often a mass of people moving as one across aisles and up and down stairways. It looked like a swarm of gnats had suddenly found a giant spotlight on a hot summer night. Indeed, the spotlight was on the man in the middle of the pack. Actor and comedian Bill Murray came to St. Paul a few times during the summer because he wanted to see the Saints, a team of which he owned one-third. The fact that he owned part of the team only served to increase its mystique in the eyes of the baseball fans of the Twin Cities, a place where the lone newspaper gossip columnist has to busy herself day after day with the petty gripes of local television news anchors because those are the most interesting celebrity goings-on she can dredge up. Bill Murray hanging around to watch a ballgame was a big, big deal. For Bill Murray, though, it was not much fun at all.

Imagine what it would be like, the next time you daydream about how great it would be to be a rich and famous movie star, to not be able to see a ballgame. Oh, you can go to the ballgame, and you could get the best seats in the house. But while the other 5,000 people in the park can kick back, order a beer and a brat, and enjoy the action, you have to cope with incessant tapping of your shoulder; items of every size and description being flung in your face, usually accompanied by a pen; and fan after well-meaning fan screaming at you their favorite lines from their favorite films you made, as if you'd forgotten you had appeared in those pictures. And heaven forbid you should stand up and try to go somewhere. That's when the gnats appear, swarming around you, hoping for you to sign their ticket stub or program or t-shirt or breast or whatever, waiting for the opportunity simply to touch you, so they can tell their friends they have had physical contact with a celebrity.

That's what it was like for Bill Murray when he tried to watch his ballclub. He was gracious about it. He signed everything, he posed for every picture, he answered questions with the acerbic wit he made famous in his movies, he nodded and smiled politely when someone shouted one of his trademark movie lines. He threw out the first ball opening night, lofting it over the backstop net into the crowd, to the screaming delight of the fans. But he was not having fun. So he eventually escaped, to the Saints dugout.

One of the joys of the Northern League as it rolled underway was its decided lack of rules, far fewer and less constricting than those of organized baseball. If the manager said it was OK, anybody who fit could spend the game in the dugout. Everyone else was in the dugout—the honorary bat boy; Adam Mosston, a producer for the ABC newsmagazine "Day One," who was working on a feature about the Saints; a guy who was writing a book about the team. So Saints manager Tim Blackwell told Murray it was just fine if he hung out with the team during the game, and while he was at it, why didn't he put on a uniform and coach first base? Murray had been a catcher in college, until he tore the rotator cuff in his shoulder, so he knew what he was doing. Why not? This was where Murray was happy. He talked to the players about baseball, about where they were from, about how they got to the Northern

League. When pen-wielding fans peeked around the corner, shouted, and begged for autographs, Murray could duck to the other end of the dugout and escape for a while. And the Saints players, who dreamed of someday being as well-known as Murray, asked him about the attention. "Oh, it's horrible," he said, dead serious now. "I'll never understand the fascination people have with my signature."

Murray felt at home because the players made him feel at home. Baseball is a curious world, a combination of the macho and the playful, where grown men endeavor to be like boys again, and they often succeed. That means that acceptance in the group is announced by childlike gestures, practical jokes, and pranks that might have earned a trip to the principal's office a few years before. So when Blackwell handed Murray a cup of water that had dribble holes punched in the bottom so he soaked his shirt, Murray knew he was welcome. When pitcher Jim Manfred stuck a four-foot stream of toilet paper out of the owner's back pocket so it fluttered behind Murray when he ran to coach first, he knew he was accepted. And when the players gave Murray a hot foot, setting his shoe on fire in the ultimate act of dugout playfulness, Murray knew he was taken in as part of the team.

Beyond the action between the foul lines, baseball is a game of atmosphere and tradition, of spontaneity and whimsy. That, in large measure, is why Miles Wolff, the Northern League's president and founder, wanted so badly to put a team in St. Paul, and why he wanted Mike Veeck to run it.

St. Paul suffers from something of an inferiority complex. It is a fairly large city, with a quarter-million people, with a rich diversity of races and ethnicities, of commercial and residential neighborhoods, of majestic mansions where a drunken F. Scott Fitzgerald used to crash dinner parties, and working class neighborhoods where families of modest means could still afford to own their own home. St. Paul has its own skyline with a handful of tall, glass-and-steel skyscrapers, a downtown shopping district with skyways to make life easier for conspicuous consumers during Minnesota's most bitter months. It has art and science museums, theaters, a zoo, even Garrison Keillor and "A Prairie Home Companion." But St. Paul lacks one thing: the name "Minneapolis." It's a badge of honor to most residents of St. Paul that they don't live in Minneapolis. That other city is larger, with more and taller shiny buildings, more shopping, more skyways, more crime and more (and more expensive) houses. It has more of just about everything—except, St. Paulites argue, more charm. And despite the teams' broad, regional names, Minneapolis is home to the Minnesota Twins, the Minnesota Vikings and the Minnesota Timberwolves. Those in St. Paul have never forgotten that.

It was therefore with no small level of satisfaction and pride that residents of St. Paul welcomed back their own professional baseball team, their first since the original St. Paul Saints, who along with the Minneapolis Millers of the Triple A American Association were booted out when the Twins arrived in 1960. Miles Wolff, then publisher of *Baseball America,* the sport's trade publication, and past owner of a gaggle of minor-league clubs, understood that history, and he understood the opportunity that came with reviving tradition and salving the ego of a community scorned. For a quarter of a million people who get steamed every time someone from out of town says, "I'm going to Minneapolis," even when he's staying at the elegant St. Paul Hotel, it would be time to gloat.

If all that wasn't enough to haul people into the park, Mike Veeck was determined to push them over the edge himself. Easy enough for a guy who was already over the edge. The name Veeck is familiar to most everybody who ever spent time studying the game, or who took a course in creative marketing. Mike's father, Bill Veeck, was to baseball what Henry Ford was to the automobile. He didn't invent it, but he made damn sure that no one had a good excuse for not becoming a customer. As owner of the minor-league Milwaukee Brewers and the major-league St. Louis Browns, Cleveland Indians and (twice) Chicago White Sox, Bill Veeck made it his mission to turn baseball into an accessible sport with a sense of humor—a task made especially difficult by his fellow owners and the commissioner of baseball, men who possessed remarkably little whimsy, considering they were charged with promoting a game. When Bill Veeck sent midget Eddie Gadel to bat for the St. Louis Browns in 1951 (Gadel walked, surprise of surprises, on four pitches), he got the attention of the world and put folks on notice that this baseball business was supposed to be a good time. He got a sharp tongue-lashing from the commissioner, the misnamed Happy Chandler, who pronounced that forthwith there would be no more midgets allowed to play in organized baseball. When you go to the park for giveaway promotions, be it ball day or seat cushion day or any other day, remember that was Bill Veeck's idea. Bill invented and had built the famous exploding scoreboard at Comiskey Park in Chicago, the precursor to today's giant color televisions that loom over baseball outfields.

When he turned serious Bill Veeck did things like sign Larry Doby, the first black to play in the American League, in 1948. And, in his final affront that led to his fellow owners ensuring that he never would own another baseball team, Veeck challenged the reserve clause. This is the instrument organized baseball has used for nearly a century to wrap its fingers around the necks of its ballplayers, to control their lives and their livelihoods, to prohibit them from leaving the company for whom they work and moving to another company, like normal people get to do. It is baseball's version of indentured servitude. Bill Veeck said as much, and that was too much for the rest of the baseball establishment. When he was concocting creative promotions and publicity stunts he was merely annoying, and the rest of the teams eventually ripped off most of his ideas anyway. But when Veeck began publicly challenging their right to the monopoly given to them by the courts and allowed to continue by Congress, he was challenging their bottom lines, and they would not have that. Veeck had to sell the White Sox to Jerry Reinsdorf and Eddie Einhorn in 1981, and his later attempts to buy the Chicago Cubs were brushed aside by the other owners as though he were a mosquito on a hot, humid day. Bill Veeck died in 1986, without a baseball team.

But like other martyrs—like the dead at the Alamo, Elvis Presley, or Obi Wan Kenobi in "Star Wars"—Veeck had become more influential in death than when he was alive. In large part, that's because his son Mike was still around and was in the baseball business. Mike Veeck, who only became close to his father in the few years before he died, liked to pretend he wasn't carrying on his dead father's legacy: "No, I don't want an exploding scoreboard here. Dad already did it. I'm not gonna do anything Dad's already done." But he really loved the comparison and did everything he could to be worthy of it. Including chatting with Dad now and then. Mike always loved making people look at him funny by recounting his discussions with his father the night before about the promotions he was considering, and how Bill would thump his peg leg once for yes and twice for no. It was one of Mike Veeck's great joys in life that he was smart enough to make people think he was a loony loose cannon, when in reality he was as calculating and deliberate as anybody who ever ran a sports franchise. It was just that what he was calculating was fun. And he was doing a pretty damn good job of it.

Of course, Mike Veeck went through a learning curve in the baseball business, just like everyone else. But, true to form, Mike's learning curve was heard throughout the baseball world with a big boom. Literally. The last time Veeck's dad owned the Chicago White Sox, he asked his son to work for him and help with promotions. Mike was young, and he would know what would draw young adults of his generation to Comiskey Park. Mike, it turns out, did his job much too well.

Mike came up with Disco Demolition, whereby a disco record and a buck would get you into the ballpark. This was 1979, the dwindling days of disco, and a Chicago disc jockey was going to blow the disco records to smithereens in between the games of a double-header. After the Sox had mashed 60,000 fans into the stadium, they had to turn 40,000 more disco haters away. "There is such a thing as a promotion that is too successful," Veeck would say later, expounding at length on Disco Demolition after briefly protesting that he didn't want to talk about it. "This one was way too successful." Indeed. After a full game of beer drinking and anticipation, the DJ did, as promised, detonate the records with a pealing boom. It was like a call to arms to the fans of rock and roll, and they poured onto the field and, in a near riot, tore up the outfield so that it looked like a farm field after the harvest. The Sox were forced to forfeit the second game, one of the few forfeits in major-league history. It was enough to make Mike infamous in the world of baseball; he would never be profiled in another newspaper or magazine without a prominent mention of Disco Demolition.

His name and his antics meant that Mike Veeck would probably never get another job in major-league baseball, but he rebounded nonetheless. A New Jersey investment banker named Marv Goldklang heard that Veeck was looking for work, and he just happened to be looking for a president for his Fort Myers Miracle, an independent team in the Single A Florida State League. It was a franchise that had always drawn poorly, and Goldklang needed someone with some good ideas that would draw folks into the stands. Veeck was his guy.

And Veeck delivered. He instituted regular gigs like putting a hair stylist in the grandstand, giving cut-rate haircuts and a view of the game. Jericho the Miracle Dog, whom Veeck met delivering sacks of groceries in a convenience store, would bring baseballs to the umpires between innings. It happens that Babe Ruth and Elvis Presley died on the same day; in honor of the occasion Veeck held Two Dead Fat Guys Night. And when an inventors' convention was in town, Mike decided to have Thomas Edison Night, a night game dedicated to the inventor of the light bulb, complete with a postgame seance to raise the dead inventor's spirit. The game was a sellout.

It's that kind of irreverence that drew Veeck to St. Paul and the Saints and the Northern League. He wanted to show the humorless suits in the Major League office suites that the game could—should—be fun, that there are enough good players out there that they miss to field a quality baseball league, and that he and others didn't need their help to do it. Veeck would rarely admit this to anyone but himself, but he also wanted to show the major leaguers that they made a mistake by shunning first his father, and then him. And he loved being the underdog.

"Nobody ever sat in the stands," he often said, "and cheered for Goliath."

Success in sports promotion is measured in two ways: the turnstile count, and the level of community awareness of a team. A club can draw plenty of fans, but if they're the same fans game after game and the team toils in relative anonymity as far as the rest of the town is concerned, that's not good promotion. Every member of the public can be aware of the team and decide not to go. That's not good promotion either. Before the season began, the Saints, with Veeck traveling from community group meeting to community group meeting, speaking to anybody who would listen, helped sell 1,100 season tickets and cut off sales, when they had hoped they might be able to sell 1,000; and they sold 800 six- and twelve-game mini packs, when they had budgeted for half that many. Mike Veeck's picture was in every newspaper and magazine in town, and every television station wanted to talk to him. When he walked around the stadium opening weekend greeting his customers, something he did every game ("Just talk to people," he said over and over. "It's not rocket science. The Twins should try it sometime."), there wasn't a soul who didn't know who he was and who didn't thank him for bringing the Saints to St. Paul. When a local church wanted to bring in more members to infuse some life into its dwindling, aging congregation, it asked Veeck to address the flock. The next morning's Minneapolis *Star Tribune* featured, in the middle of its front page, a photo of Veeck at the pulpit, with his arms outstretched, looking like the second coming of P.T. Barnum, telling a full house that they should print religious trading cards: "Joseph. Bats left, throws right."

Now *that's* good promotion.

CHAPTER THREE

The Key to
the Batter's Box

As the Saints' first homestand progressed, a phenomenon was occurring. It was something similar to those circles that kept appearing in wheat fields in England: a lot of people could come up with plenty of different theories about what was happening, but it was probably best to just sit back and watch it unfold. Maybe as time went on the explanation would become more clear. Everybody expected the home opener would sell out, though few expected it to happen within an hour after tickets went on sale. And it was reasonable to suppose that the rest of that first three-game series might draw well. And, sure, by the time opening day rolled around, there were hardly any unsold reserved seats for the rest of the season, leaving only general admission— three bucks for a space on a slab of metal and all the sun you can soak up—that was not beyond the realm of anyone's comprehension. But beyond that, when ticket manager Stephanie Baumgartner (actually, she had been hired several months earlier to answer phones. She was drafted into this job of managing the flow of tickets for the best-drawing team in the minor leagues, and she often wished she were back answering phones again) opened the floodgates every day two hours before game time, there was a line that extended from the box-office window, back down the three steps on the terrace fifty feet back, and all the way past the hundred-foot cement wall that separated the stadium entrance area from the grass below leading to the Saints' offices. The games sold out.

It was that way on June 23, as a full house listed at 5,069 (really it was closer to 5,300 or 5,400) wedged themselves into their seats and waited for the game to begin against the Duluth-Superior Dukes. Most incredible about this draw, probably, was that these folks had ignored the fore-cast cal-ling for heavy evening thunderstorms, and they now paid little attention to the sinister dark clouds roiling overhead. The air was thick and damp, and it had that musty, tempestuous smell that preceded a torrent. They wanted to see a ballgame, dammit, and this was the one they were going to see.

Or maybe not. The Dukes were unable to produce in the top of the first inning, but the Saints managed to put two on base in their half of the first. With two out, and with everybody feeling pretty smug that they were able to sneak this game in under the nose of the thunderstorm bully, the base umpire suddenly ordered everybody off the field. From his vantage point looking southwest, from where Municipal Stadium weather originates, he saw lightning strikes on the horizon. The rule is clear: If lighting is in the area, where it can reach lighting standards and metal bleachers and the baseball players and fans, the game will be suspended.

It was a fine idea, for within five minutes of the teams clearing the field the skies opened. This was no ordinary shower, either. Water was coming down with the ferocity generally associated with waterfalls, not precipitation. Never mind the fact that this deluge continued for only fifteen minutes. It was a quarter-hour of tremendous rain-fall, more than even Municipal Stadium—a ballpark built with drainage in mind—could withstand. As fans in the stands battled in water fights, kicking puddles of standing rainwater on each other as they ran through the grand-stand, the umpires decided the game would be sus-pended until the following night, as part of a double-header. The first $25,000 gate of the year was lost because they forgot to dome Municipal Stadium.

○ ○ ○

"Suspended" seems a simple enough term. Ask Webster's: it means "to delay an action or proceeding." That means you pick up where you left off. The rule books are equally clear: if a game is suspended, it resumes in the same inning, with the same number of outs, the same count on the same batter, the same runners on the same bases. But Duluth manager Mal Fichman works with a different version of the English language than the rest of us. Seems Mal wanted the game to start over. It was simple logic, he said, and the fact that his team would take the field with Saints runners on second and third was immaterial. And he argued the case, in person and over the phone, with Miles Wolff and Northern League executive director Tom Leip, until he had driven nuts anybody who had the bad fortune to be within earshot. After three minutes or so, Mal lost his case, and he announced to all that he was playing the game under protest because of it.

Should it come as a surprise to you that Mal Fichman was not well-liked around the Northern League? Actually, he was not a big favorite anywhere in baseball. He had bounced around baseball for years, scouting for major-league clubs here and there, and managing average teams in the rookie Pioneer League, but not much else. A diminutive, frumpy man, Mal stood about five-foot-five in thick socks, and in his Dukes uniform he looked horribly out of place, his pants legs too long, the extra fabric bunching up around his butt, his hat perched high atop his head as though he forgot to push it down far enough, the baseball-sized wad of chew forever lodged in his cheek so you could almost see him getting cancer of the gums as he stood there. Though his appearance was striking in its shabbiness, it was Mal the man that made so many people like him so little. Ask Kent Blasingame, Saints outfielder, who should have and could have been a Dukes outfielder. Mal did more than express interest in Kent, son of former major leaguer Don Blasingame, after a Northern League tryout camp in California. He offered him a contract. Kent found a place to live in Duluth. Then Fichman, in a pattern he repeated many times in a shady effort to stock his roster while having to pay as few players as possible, withdrew the offer. Blasingame was fortunate: he latched on with St. Paul. Others weren't as lucky.

Mal's modus operandi extended to his selection of a pitching coach. Mitch Zwolensky was a known quantity in the baseball world. This tall, imposing, graying coach had washed out the previous year as a pitching coach for Stockton, the Milwaukee Brewers' Single A team in the California League, but not before developing a significant reputation as a nasty operator who thought nothing of having his pitchers throw at batters' heads just to back them off the plate. It's not a pitching philosophy that endears one to opposing teams, and Blackwell was ready for Zwolensky to try it.

"This guy wants his pitchers to hit people," Blackwell warned his players in the dugout before the doubleheader. "He wants to scare guys. He wants you to wonder, when you step up to the plate, whether you're going to get hit or not. I'm not talking about brushing you back to back you off the plate, I'm talking about hitting guys."

Ed Stryker knew. The Saints reliever pitched the last two years with Bakersfield, the Los Angeles Dodgers' entry in the California League. Zwolensky's reputation was legend there, he said. "When the count is oh-and-two, he comes right in on you."

Sure enough, Rick Hirtensteiner, the Saints' leadoff hitter, got plunked right in the small of the back. Then Tommy Raffo came to the plate and took a pitch off his wrist. When the home-plate umpire awarded him first base, Fichman raised a tremendous fuss, maintaining that the ball had actually hit Raffo's hand, which, according to the rules, is considered part of the bat, which would have made that a foul ball. Fichman, apparently, had no explanation for the silver dollar-sized welt on Raffo's wrist. Then Zwolensky came out, ostensibly to talk to his pitcher. But as he strode to the mound, crossing the first-base foul line, he was screaming at the umpire. "It hit his fucking hand! It hit his fucking hand! Why don't you watch next time?" The fans still tailgating in the parking lot could hear his shrieking.

Stryker couldn't believe Zwolensky was allowed to remain in the game after that. "He just embarrassed that ump in front of five thousand people. You've got to run his ass for that."

But the day was not done, and neither was the antagonism between Duluth and St. Paul. In the second game, in the bottom of the second, with Scott Meadows on first, Blasingame bunted. Actually, Kent Blasingame almost always bunted. Fully one-third of his hits this year would be bunt singles. There was never any mystery about Blasingame's intentions; the third baseman would shuffle halfway down the line towards home plate, the first baseman would dart in, and Kent would still square to bunt. This time, pitcher Doug Tegtmeier, covering first, dropped the ball, and Blasingame was safe on one of his trademark (and unnecessary) headfirst slides into first base. He stood up to brush himself off, but the pitcher, still fuming over his error that allowed the base to be occupied in the first place, would not vacate the bag. Instead, he nudged Blasingame. Kent pushed back, and the melee was on.

It's a baseball ritual that when two players begin pushing and shoving, both teams pour onto the field to join the fray. It's rare that anybody ever actually hits anybody else, except possibly for the two people who started the whole thing in the first place, but loyalty to one's teammates requires a ballplayer to get out and grab the collar of someone wearing a different-colored uniform. That was the case here, except for Tim Blackwell. A devout Christian and an even-tempered, mild-mannered guy, Blackwell is not normally given to throttling anybody. But he sprinted the length of the field, and when he got to first base he picked out Zwolensky from the mob and tightly fastened his hands around the pitching coach's neck, until a couple of Blackwell's players pried him loose.

Duluth didn't throw at any Saints for the rest of the series.

○ ○ ○

Fans of minor-league baseball often look for examples of why their game is different from the major leagues, and why their version is better. In the Northern League's inaugural season this search for explanations took on new importance, since this was an entity that needed to prove itself, and it didn't have a sugar daddy like a major-league parent club to help it along. In organized baseball, farm teams get their players from the parent club, which can keep them there or yank them out at will. Fans are reluctant to develop loyalties to favorite players then, since their hero might be told that night to pack his bags and move to the next level. In return, the major-league club picks up the tab for player salaries, insurance, and other expenses. It's like when your folks give you an allowance, but as long as you live under their roof, you are going to follow their rules, and they don't want to hear another word about it. The Northern League is the sixteen-year-old who left home to make it on his own. Nobody thinks he can do it, but he's doggedly determined to try, and after all those years of watching how his mom and dad operate, he figures he can learn from their mistakes and to capitalize on their strong points. He feels pretty sure he's ready to head out alone.

One of the Northern League's biggest drawing cards in its first year was accessibility to its players. Fans could get close to the players, collect autographs, talk, take players out to dinner, and unlike many teams in organized baseball, the Northern League had few rules about who could talk to whom when. As long as the fans didn't interfere with the game, they were free to fraternize. On the Saints' first trip to Rochester, June 25 and 26, a group of 10-year-olds learned just that. Jon Hanson, Joe Kelley, and David Young simply walked through the dugout door at Mayo Park as the team was waiting for its turn in batting practice. And just like every other kid in every town, they asked for baseballs. But they asked intelligently. "We'll get you a Coke," they offered. So for every autographed baseball they collected, Jon and Joe and David would troop back to the Rochester Aces party area, where they were part of a group having a cookout before the game, ask for a soft drink from the Aces employee charged with giving them free to the partygoers who had rented the picnic area, and take them back to the players. A dozen pops later, the three boys had an impressive collection of autographed balls that seriously depleted the Saint's ball bucket.

Mayo Park in Rochester is a curious place. Named for the same guy as the clinic (half the structures in town have "Mayo" somewhere in their names), this stadium has long been a home for high school and American Legion ball, but it was never intended for professional baseball. Pro ballplayers can hit the ball too far. The stated dimensions are 390 to straight center and 310 down the baselines. That's like saying a ten-story building is fifteen floors high, or that the interstate speed limit is seventy-five miles an hour. It's overstating the case just a bit. Even Rochester general manager Doug Stewart admitted it. "It's more like three hundred down the lines. Hey, we don't lead the league in home runs for nothing." That's right Doug, except it's more like 290. A medium pop fly down either baseline is a four-bagger. During St. Paul's batting practice, Eddie Ortega was knocking balls out of the yard, and Ortega doesn't even have warning-track power in most parks. He has something closer to 20-feet-short-of-the-warning-track power. During one of the Saints' slugfests at Mayo (there's no such thing as a pitcher's duel at this park), Jim Eppard took a ball out to right. Eppard was a baseball player of many fine talents, but power was not one of them. If he took you deep, you knew your park is too small.

There weren't that many seats at Mayo Park, either. Stated seating capacity there was 2,500, though there didn't seem to be room for 2,500 rear ends on those bleachers. No one may ever know, though, because the Aces never drew well enough to test its capacity. With an affluent metropolitan area of around 100,000, bursting to overflowing with Mayo Clinic doctors and IBM engineers who worked at the company's giant Rochester facility, and located ninety minutes southwest of the Twin Cities, Rochester would seem to be the perfect place for a minor-league franchise.

Couple of problems, though. First, Rochester also played host to the Rochester Renegade, a Continental Basketball Association franchise that the winter before could probably claim the title of worst professional basketball team on the planet, winning all of five games. No one was going to shell out good money on the possibility that this baseball team might play just as poorly. Second, the team was owned by Charles Sanders, a nice, capable man who was a former vice president for the Atlanta Braves. But Sanders lived in Atlanta. He didn't understand Rochester, he had never been there before he started the franchise, and he only popped in occasionally once the season began. Sanders had a perfectly capable general manager with a competent staff running the team in his absence, but the top-down attitude that was translated to the community was one that said, "Congratulations, your town has been awarded a professional baseball franchise. Go see some games."

The electric atmosphere that prevailed at other Northern League parks—especially in St. Paul, and to a lesser extent in places like Duluth and Thunder Bay—was missing in Rochester. There were a couple of between-inning promotions (Sioux Falls had the best, where two Canaries tried to knock out a car's headlights with thrown baseballs to win twenty-five bucks each for them and a designated fan) and some lucky-number program giveaways, but there was never a feeling of synergy or the knowledge you were someplace special. Local ownership would have helped, but Miles Wolff made a conscious decision to avoid local ownership. He had seen enough poorly run, locally owned teams in his decades in minor-league baseball to know he wanted people running his show that had experience in the game, and that would run solid baseball operations first, parties second. In Rochester that philosophy hurt the club, and the league. This was the one club that would not at least break even in the league's inaugural season; the stated average attendance was around 1,500 a game, but that came from the Late Chicago Mayor Richard Daley School of Creative Counting (motto: "Vote early and often"). There were usually fewer than 1,000 people in the stands on those 1,500 nights, and since this was a club that sold fewer than 500 season tickets, one wondered where they were getting these counts from anyway.

"Hey, Brandon, could you go get me the key to the batter's box?"

"Where is it?"

"I don't know, I haven't seen it all day. Ask around."

The Saints clubhouse manager Brent Proulx, in cahoots with trainer Dave Fricke, had begun initiating batboy Brandon Martin. The batter's box, of course, is nothing but a rectangular chalk outline beside home plate, but when you're a fifteen-year-old kid who gets to hang around professional baseball players and do their bidding, you obey first and consider whether you're looking for something absurd later.

So Brandon looked. And he asked. He asked Blackwell, and Eppard, and most of the rest of the Saints players. He asked Fanning. He asked Veeck. He figured maybe the key was over at the visitor's clubhouse, so he asked the Thunder Bay trainer, and then manager Dan Schwam. That's the great thing about baseball gags: none of them are new, so everybody knows them. It's understood in the game, just as much as how everybody knows to throw the ball around the horn to start an inning, that when someone is looking for the key to the batter's box—or for the box of curveballs, or for the left-handed bats—that you look at him with a perfectly straight face and say, "Geez, I haven't seen it lately. Why don't you ask (Fill in the blank, preferably with someone at the other end of the stadium)."

Leon Durham knows. He even felt a certain measure of sympathy for Brandon as he went on his chase for a full half-hour before he finally figured it out. "They got me with that in the major leagues, when I was a rookie," he remembered. "It took me an hour to figure it out. Everybody was laughing so hard they almost fell over."

And he told Brandon so—*after* Brandon had figured it out.

○ ○ ○

It was a clear, cool Monday evening, this June 28, with the batter's box securely unlocked and the Saints sitting three games up in first place with a 9-2 record. The stands at Municipal Stadium were filling with fans, and the TV stations had their live trucks set up to give the Saints faithful the details of their next triumph at the earliest possible moment. It was enough to make a manager feel downright giddy, even if his team was down 6-0 by the end of the second inning.

"I'll tell you what," Blackwell called to his corps as he paced on the outside of the chain-link mesh, "we've got them right where we want them. They're feeling good now, but they're going to be awfully surprised when we come back and beat them. They're just sitting back, taking it easy."

At that point, the Jacks could afford to. After losing six straight on the road to open the season—including three of the Saints' first six victories—the Whiskey Jacks sauntered up to their crisp home on the north shore of Lake Superior and promptly won six straight to bring their record up to .500. In Thunder Bay, the support of the Whiskey Jacks' fans had to have something to do with their success. For their home opener, the team voted most likely to fall on its face, the one that couldn't beg folks to buy more than 500 season tickets, drew 6,200 to its first game. In a 4,500-seat park. No mirrors. Illusionist David Copperfield was nowhere to be seen. But there were folks spread out three-deep along the warning track in fair territory, where they were a ground-rule double if hit. Jacks' center fielder Rodney McCray made one catch fading back towards the crowd, stepped gingerly between two fans' Molsons, turned and threw back to the infield. You've got to win home games in a place like that.

But the Thunder Bay fans had nothing to do with the way the Whiskey Jacks played this Monday. They just plain beat the Saints. John Thoden, who entered the game with a 0.83 earned run average, did serious damage to that statistic by giving up six earned runs on nine hits over three innings. The Saints never did catch up the way Blackwell had predicted.

"Where's Brent? Hey, Brent, that coffee hasn't kicked in for anybody yet. Go get some more."

Enough of that. The Saints were poised for a big night June 30. They were still in first place, the club everybody needed to beat. The Famous Chicken was in town to amuse the crowd with his well-known antics, the game was a sellout, and the Saints controlled their own destiny. Only the St. Paul Saints would determine how they would play this night.

Wrong. In the summer of 1993, the rain never seemed to stop. Farmers lost their crops. Families lost their homes. Des Moines was without drinking water for weeks. Levees broke and the Mississippi and Missouri rivers overflowed their banks with an enthusiasm that bade poorly for the economic health of the nation's midsection. It seemed unimportant then, that the St. Paul Saints would be bummed out at the prospect of yet another lost gate, even one that included the Chicken's rainout fee of $2,500 (he would have gotten $6,000 if he had actually performed). But this was still a game and was, by definition, trivial, even if this little bit of trivia meant thousands of dollars lost for the St. Paul Saints Baseball Club.

"Normally I'm not a man given to cursing, but I'm very close right now," muttered Marv Goldklang after he got off the phone with the National Weather Service and realized this game would not be played. The Chicken was in the main concourse autographing pictures for the fans who stuck around—something he didn't have to do under his contract, but this was one friendly chicken—and the grounds crew was on the field trying to save the pitcher's mound and the home plate area from floating away down Energy Park Drive. It was another thirty grand out of the team's pocket.

But don't believe Goldklang about the cursing part. A soft-spoken man worth millions of dollars, but with so little pretension that you would never know it unless you saw his bank book, Goldklang didn't swear even when he was enraged. And he was not angry now. In fact, he was in a darned good mood, downright giddy. Considering the team's biggest promotion of the year was just washed away, never to be seen again.

Goldklang could thank the Minnesota Twins for his good humor; there was very little the Saints could thank the Twins for (besides playing in the Metrodome), so Marv's beatitude was doubly curious. "Did you hear the Twins' new radio advertisement?" he asked, bounding down the runway from the office to the field. "The Twins are running a radio advertisement—I heard it, Mike Veeck heard it—that says, why sit amongst the bugs, dealing with the rain? Come to the Metrodome, where it's comfortable.

"We're getting to them."

Mike Veeck will tell you that while he is proud of his father's legacy, he is not eager to continue it; rather, Mike would like to strike out on his own, separate himself from his dad and not be thought of in the same breath.

Not likely.

Just ask Minnie Minoso. Like Larry Doby, the first black American League player, and Max Patkin, who has made his living for forty years as baseball's "Clown Prince," Minoso owes his baseball career to Bill Veeck. Veeck signed Doby with the Cleveland Indians to break the final baseball color barrier, and two decades later he hired Doby to manage the Chicago White Sox. He hired Patkin to coach for the St. Louis Browns and encouraged him to make ample use of his rubbery features and looney sense of humor, and Mike Veeck has brought Patkin into his ballpark every season to this day, even though Max is more embarrassing than funny at age seventy-two. And Bill Veeck gave Minoso his first shot in the major leagues, and he did everything he could to give the aging legend his shot at baseball immortality. Finally, Mike was able to help with that, too. Minoso broke into professional baseball in 1946, with the New York Cubans. He completed a distinguished professional career with the Indians, White Sox, Philadelphia A's, St. Louis

Cardinals, and Washington Senators, until 1964. Then, to make Minoso the first man to play professional baseball during five decades, Bill Veeck put a uniform on Minoso and sent him to bat for the White Sox in 1976 and 1980. Mike Veeck, ever his father's son, tried to hold up the legacy by having Minoso appear in a game for his Miami Miracle in 1990.

SCREECH! Put on the brakes. This is baseball, a dignified game. We can't have somebody like Mike Veeck make a mockery of the national pastime by fielding an old man pushing seventy. So thank heavens then-commissioner Fay Vincent stepped in and, in the best interests of baseball, put a stop to this Minnie Minoso business. Let the guy go away quietly like so many other aging ballplayers. Doesn't he have an autograph show to attend? Get on with the game.

But the Veecks are a loyal lot, and they don't forget much. Mike never forgot how White Sox owners Eddie Einhorn and Jerry Reinsdorf forced his father out of baseball and into ridicule. Just the same, he never forgot how organized baseball has always seemed to stand in the way of a Veeck having fun at a baseball game, or trying to help others have fun as well. But this time, there was no Fay Vincent or Happy Chandler or Bud Selig. Miles Wolff ran this show, and he specifically recruited Mike Veeck so he would pull stunts like this. Minnie Minoso was in the best interests of the Northern League, no question about it. So this seventy-year-old man, who with his taut body and leathery, rugged, dark face could easily pass for fifteen years younger, sat himself down in front of an open locker in the home team clubhouse at Municipal Stadium, put himself in a Saints uniform, and headed for the dugout. Minnie Minoso was back, and he was in the lineup.

That, of course, was after the signing ceremony. Mike Veeck would never let a happening like this go by without collecting the proper attention from the proper media outlets. With the television cameras rolling, Mike speechified about how he was going to send this contract to Cooperstown, since the Hall of Fame won't put Minoso there as a player. "If anything, or any gentleman deserves to be in

Cooperstown, it is this man," Veeck intoned with an important look on his face. The seriousness lasted for about twenty seconds, the longest Mike Veeck has ever been recorded holding a scowl. "I guess Fay isn't here to stop us this time."

Minnie started the game at designated hitter, batting second, standing in against Yoshi Seo, a nineteen-year-old Japanese import who was busily confounding Northern League hitters with his nasty slider and his ability to change speeds on his pitches. No one could touch him. And no one knew what to expect when Minoso stepped up to the plate. He looked good, but he was seventy years old. What if a pitch came at his head? Would he still have the reaction time to get out of the way? Does he have any intention of even taking the bat off his shoulder? There was as much apprehension and concern about this at-bat as there was curiosity.

But Minnie Minoso made history without embarrassing himself; indeed, he didn't look all that bad. He sent a 2-0 fastball bounding back toward the mound, where Seo scooped it up and threw out Minoso, who was running all the way.

And the commissioner of baseball was not even chasing him.

CHAPTER FOUR

Hip Waders and Diamond Rings

The image most people have of professional base-ball—the portrait they get from watching major-league operations in action—is one of cool, professional competence, of an assembly of workers, each with his or her own task, doing it well and efficiently. The fully-staffed grounds crew tending to the infield and outfield, making sure they are in perfect playing condition; the media relations office handling interview and press pass requests and gathering facts and figures for that day's game; the sales staff working to secure sponsorship for promotions and advertising and seeing to it those agreements come off without a hitch; the concession department making sure all the food, drink and souvenirs are well-stocked, fresh and ready to sell; the ticket office, calmly and in an organized fashion processing all the fans who want to see the game that day and on days to come; and the general manager, coordinating it all in a statespersonlike and authoritative fashion.

That bucolic image is razed after one day with a minor-league organization. Everybody does whatever needs to be done to make sure the game is played and the things that need to be sold are indeed sold. If a phone is ringing, the one closest to it answers, whether that person is Mike Veeck or the person actually hired to answer phones. Dave Wright, who holds the title media relations director, will be only too happy to sell you a program ad or a season ticket. And on July 3, 1993, at Municipal Stadium, any illusion anyone might have had about a division of labor would have been sloshed away in a river of rainwater.

Rochester was in town for the holiday weekend; the Fourth fell on a Sunday, and Saturday was the day for the Saints' gala fireworks display, promising to be about as subdued as anything Mike Veeck has ever done, so both Saturday's and Sunday's games were sold out, and had been for days. A sellout brings in close to $25,000 in ticket revenue, not to mention the thousands more all those fans will spend on hot dogs, peanuts, beer, sweatshirts, and hats. For an organization whose original budget was $650,000 (which, incidentally, was $400,000 *less* than the average annual major-league salary for one player), a sellout was an important component to a fiscally successful season.

So never mind the rain that came that morning, starting about 10:30. The steady, pelting downpour came and stayed, stalling over Municipal Stadium like the perennial rain cloud that hovered over the Addams Family's house in the old TV show. The storm overstayed its welcome, hanging around for three and a half hours, finally clearing out as quickly as it came and leaving in its wake a brilliant sun and a downright pleasant seventy-eight degrees. It also left a new body of water, Lake Warning Track, which began to breed its own ecosystem along the outfield wall, up to a foot deep in some spots, from one foul line to the other.

Even after the rain stopped and the sun began drying the field five hours before game time, the ticket-holders began calling. "You're not going to play tonight, are you?" they asked again and again in the soft, anxious whine that comes from too many years of never seeing a baseball game outside, where the weather could even be a factor. They knew the answer would be no. They should be playing in the damned Dome. "Oh, we're playing," Bill Fanning said, whenever anyone asked him. "That's not even an option."

It was a display of confidence from Fanning that was brought on more from an intense desire to hold onto a sold-out gate rather than from any real optimism that the field would be ready by game time. Fanning, Wright, intern John Spolyer, the sales staff of Peter Orme, Dan Craighead, and Tom Whaley, as well as the entire grounds crew, began as soon as the rains stopped to divert the flow of water as it settled along the outfield wall and extended well past the warning track onto the outfield grass. Even if the Minnesota Twins played outdoors, you'd never see Twins general manager Andy MacPhail as Fanning was this day, hip waders pulled over faded jeans, wearing a worn T-shirt, and with a fat wad of chew firmly embedded in his cheek, wielding a shovel and digging drainage ditches in the warning track to guide the water through holes dug under the right-center field wall that led to another drainage ditch, and finally, mercifully ended up in a storm sewer. Fanning was a thirty-eight-year-old former college baseball player, who gave up a lucrative life as a banker and a stockbroker to work in baseball, taking mid-level front office jobs with minor-league clubs in Denver, Spokane, and Wichita, before winding up running the show in St. Paul, all for the privilege of learning how to work a sump pump under a bright blue sky.

The pumps were necessary because the drainage ditches, while clever and mildly effective, would not dry the field in time for autumn, let alone for that night's ballgame. So Dave Wright gave up media relations that afternoon and went to a local rental shop, which provided him with two sump pumps, devices that Wright had never seen in person before, let alone used. "I've heard of them before," Dave explained, "I just didn't know what they did." The Northern League was nothing if not educational. Wright and the others learned quickly, though, as they began what turned out to be three straight hours of pumping, starting at center field and working their way towards right, until by the time they stopped ten minutes before game time, only a few small puddles remained, and they were ready to play ball.

But were the Saints themselves ready to play ball? When the team won its first six in a row and nine of its first eleven, the St. Paul Saints seemed a club of destiny. Everybody got along, went out together at home and on the road, joked around before and during the games, and exuded confidence. Tim Blackwell and player-coach Jim Eppard noted more than once after early victories how it took the team a good half-hour or more to shower and change after a victory. "When I was in Columbia, everybody would be out of here within 15 minutes, and we were winning," remembered Blackwell of his two New York Mets-affiliated championship teams in the Single A South Atlantic League. "That tells me we have good chemistry here. But let's see if it continues when we've lost a few." When you're winning, you feel that you ought to be winning, like there is no good reason for you to lose. It makes you play that much better; winning begets winning, and that's how the St. Paul Saints began their inaugural season. But winning can also beget overconfidence and sloppy play. And St. Paul did eventually lose those few that Blackwell was waiting for.

They had lost 11-9 in Rochester the day before, wasting a home run and four RBI by Durham, an Eppard home run (something that almost never happens), and fourteen hits overall when reliever Paul Marak came on in the seventh and promptly gave up a pinch-hit grand slam to Darrin Dreasky, who was batting in the ninth spot in the order. That was the Saints' second straight loss, dropping their record to 10-5; they had lost three of their last four, and five of their last ten. Tim Blackwell is a pretty even-tempered guy, but he was sick of managing what he knew was the most talented team in the Northern League and getting stomped on every night.

Before the game on July 3, as the entire front office was working furiously to dry the field and the sellout crowd was filing into the stands, Blackie was stalking the dugout. It's difficult to really tell Blackwell's emotions just by looking at him—his overgrowth of mustache does much to mask his facial expressions—but it was clear this was an unhappy and impatient man, one who wanted his team to pick up the pace and show a little emotion. "C'mon, let's win a game this month! Let's hear some chatter out there. Do we need to get a designated cheering section in here? Let's get something started. I'll go out and get a pair of pom-poms myself if I have to."

The Saints managed to squeak through that game with an 8-6 win, but it was ugly, and Blackwell was still not happy.

When Rick Hirtensteiner—normally one of the most alert and intelligent players on the team—missed a steal sign after hitting a single, it was at least the third such lapse of the game. Blackwell trotted over to the St. Paul dugout, threw up his hands, and asked nobody in particular, "Am I going too fast on those signs? Can you see my signs?" Then he trotted back out to the third-base coach's box.

The Saints were 11-6, and their ironclad, sure-thing, set-in-stone, bet-the-farm lock on a wire-to-wire first-place run had quickly, quietly slipped away. They were in a tie for the league lead with the Thunder Bay Whiskey Jacks.

There's very little the St. Paul Saints would not have done for a gag during their first season; the wilder the better, and preferably it would be something that nobody had tried before. That's why the team had a pig bringing the balls out to the umpires, why fans could have pizzas from a local restaurant delivered to them in the stands, get a massage or a haircut, and why, when the song got to the line about "Buy me some peanuts and Cracker Jack," the folks in the press box would do just that, throwing the bags and boxes out the open window to the frenzied crowd below. So when Jared Rosati called the Saints office on July 3 and said he wanted to propose to his girlfriend the following day, and could the club possibly flash the message on the scoreboard between innings, the team would have none of that. Instead, Mike Veeck instructed his crew to begin efforts immediately to secure a helicopter. The plan, as Veeck envisioned it in his foggy world of virtual reality, was to have the chopper land in center field, disgorge Rosati and have him charge up into the stands to where Dina Hackett was waiting, slipping the diamond ring on her finger as the throng of ever-romantic Saints fans erupted in ecstasy and the two lovers embraced in eternal love.

Two problems: first, the scheme lacked the innocence and spontaneity that should mark such a soft and tender moment as a marriage proposal, the infinite moment when a man and a woman declare their intention to commit to everlasting love and togetherness. It should be an instant of shimmering recognition, but it would be ruined by the dragging moments between the time Jared hopped from the bird and was recognized by his intended and when he finally arrived at her seat (perhaps out of breath) to pop the question. Second, they couldn't get a helicopter on such short notice.

No, the St. Paul Saints promotion brain trust would have to use its wits, to dig deep in the vault of originality and come up with something novel enough to hold fan interest, and sneaky enough so they could pull it off as a total surprise to an unsuspecting Dina. Intern John "Brown and Serve" Spolyer saved the day. Called Brown for short, John earned his nickname from his technique of unashamed, unabashed, unadulterated brown-nosing. He would do virtually anything for just about anybody if it would earn him points (Brown was best known around Municipal Stadium for his oft-uttered query, "Can I get you anything?"). More often it earned him dubious honors like the nickname "Brown and Serve," but he did work hard, and he deserved full credit for this notion.

When the team's customer-service whiz Annie Huidekoper—whose job it was to do everything to make sure whatever happened before the game, and in the stands during the game, went off without trouble—told them of the plan and asked for their help, Blackwell and the Saints' players could barely contain themselves, so zealously did they offer assistance. One discernible difference between the Northern League and other, affiliated, minor leagues was that Northern Leaguers were not afraid to have a little fun, the Saints probably more than anybody. The relaxed, affable clubhouse atmosphere made Jared Rosati feel at home; still, when some players asked him in concert if he was nervous, he shook his head rapidly as if to clear it. "Nervous, me? Holy fuck yes."

Rosati, Hackett, Rosati's brother, and a few of their friends got their reserved seats—a precious commodity at Saints games, especially in bunches of six—from a "friend" Jared had working in the Saints office (true, in as much as anybody who helps Veeck pull off a gag is automatically a buddy for life). Of course, Jared had to head for the press box well before game time to visit his friend. Really, he went down to the clubhouse and began changing into a Saints uniform. Stephane Dionne brought over his catchers gear, the whole set: knee pads, chest protector, helmet, mask glove. Everything but the cup, which Jared figured he probably wouldn't need anyway. When Jared put the whole thing on, it might as well have been anybody behind that getup. Meanwhile, Dina and their friends were oblivious to the goings-on in the locker room. They had no idea Tim Blackwell had approached Jared, closely inspecting Dina's great-grandmother's diamond engagement ring—a massive setting of stones bought and paid for in a simpler and less expensive time—leaned over to Jared, raised his eyebrows, and noted, "After all this, she'd better say yes." Dina, working on her tan in Section B, Row PP, with her purple striped tank top and shorts, just thought she was going to watch a ballgame, and she wanted to know where her boyfriend was.

Her boyfriend still didn't show up, but Mike Veeck did. By a remarkable coincidence, he selected Dina to throw out the first pitch as part of a special Saints Fourth of July promotion, designed to show that in America, Land of the Free, anyone could be selected to throw out the first pitch at a ballgame. Actually, the gag almost fell apart right there, since Veeck at first couldn't find Dina, then almost picked the wrong tank-top-clad woman. But Dina was a good sport, just as Jared predicted she would be, and she allowed herself to be coaxed through the runway beneath the stands and onto the field.

As Annie escorted Dina to the mound, out came the catcher, in full battle dress, ready to backstop the ceremonial first ball. He placed himself behind home plate, crouched, and put his mitt out to make a target for which Dina could aim. She wound and fired, sending a one-hopper to the plate, which the catcher fielded cleanly. He jogged out to the mound to his blank-faced love and, just before he reached the clay hill, took off his mask. Dina's expression remained blank for just a moment until she realized who this man really was, and she registered the shock that comes with the totally unexpected, and that makes an event like this such a joy to watch. Jared dropped the ball she had thrown and handed her another from his pocket. Next to "Official Northern League Ball, Miles Wolff, president," the Magic Marker scribbling read, "Dina, will you marry me? Jared." Then he pulled the other thing out of his back pocket: the ring, which Dina didn't even know he had. She wasn't sure whether to laugh or to cry, so she compromised, gasping a speechless stream of disbelief, throwing her arms around her man. They walked, arm-in-arm, laughing and crying, off the field.

She said yes.

CHAPTER FIVE

The Difference Between Losing and Getting Beat

Whatever glamour life as a minor-league baseball player might appear to have, it disappears about halfway through the first long road trip. This is when the allure is stripped away like layers of paint off the walls of an old building. You scrape and scrape and scrape, looking for the charm you are sure is hiding underneath, only to get closer with each layer to the crumbling plaster. The reality is the long bus rides, making $15 a day in meal money stretch far enough to feed a calorie-hungry athlete, the days and nights alone, with only a snoring teammate in the next bed to keep you company in another hotel room that suffers from chronic sameness with the one the night before, and the one on the trip before that. People tend to extrapolate the glitz of big-league road life—the chartered planes; first-class hotels; $75 per diems for food that fawning fans and thankful restaurant owners often buy for you anyway, so happy are they to have celebrities in their midst; the flunkies there to carry your bags—but they don't realize the minor leagues have none of that.

This was plainly clear the morning of July 5, when the St. Paul Saints dragged themselves to the stadium at seven o'clock, as the sun was still groaning its way into the eastern sky beyond the right field wall—a time when most of the players are just about entering REM sleep on normal days —to catch the bus for their first week-long road trip, to Sioux City and Duluth. The foremost thoughts on most players' minds, once they gathered their own equipment bags from the clubhouse and lugged them and their suitcases into the lower cargo holds of the motorcoach, were finding their seats and going back to sleep. The Saints normally traveled with between twenty-five and twenty-seven people, and there were only twenty-two pairs of velour-covered, rusty brown, barely-reclining seats on the bus. Having two seats to oneself was a luxury accorded to those with stature (Blackwell), seniority (Durham), or quiet determination and getting to the bus early (Rick Hirtensteiner). Comfort was where you could find it, and Eddie Ortega and Willie Smith, two of the more diminutive Saints, discovered it in the overhead luggage racks, where they could stretch out and rest. Kent Blasingame found the same on the aisle floor. Between Kent splayed underfoot and half the rest of the team creatively reposed across the aisle and over armrests, getting from the front of the coach to the bathroom at the rear was an adventure in creative climbing, bounding from one armrest to the next, one's feet never touching the ground.

Manager Blackwell, player-coach Eppard, and trainer Fricke (and nine-year-old twins Michael and Matthew Blackwell, when they traveled with the team), held court in the first two rows, with Blackwell taking the front seat on the right, Eppard on the left, and Fricke (it's pronounced with a long "E", like "quickie") behind Blackwell. They would consult on important matters concerning the team: who was playing well, who wasn't, and what they should do about it; game strategy; whom to pitch when. They would discuss the myriad of details that come with running a minor-league ballclub, like travel arrangements, personality conflicts among players, and arranging for late-checkout hotel rooms, so the players have a place to go after the noon checkout time but before the 4:15 p.m. bus to the park on the last day in a city. Picture a dozen and a half ballplayers, squeezed on two beds and sprawled on the floor amongst all their luggage, watching a Cubs game on TV and doing bad Harry Caray imitations ("And here's Jose Vish-caooon. . . .And it's a drive! It could be, it could be, it is!"). They would trade stories of their years in baseball; they would talk about gardening and relatives.

On this morning the three (minus the twins) were discussing the fortunes of the St. Paul Saints in the first half of the seventy-two-game season; Blackwell noted that after their meteoric beginning, the team was now 11-6 at the midpoint of the first half. "Yeah," Epp noted, "and we've only been beat twice."

It was true. Marv Goldklang was an investment banker by vocation but a baseball lover by avocation who was fortunate enough to have the means to immerse himself into his hobby not through the normal channels of fantasy baseball leagues and Wednesday night softball leagues, but by actually owning his own teams. At that point, he owned all or part of four minor-league clubs, one Australian League team and a minority share of the New York Yankees (he had invested in parts of other clubs in the past). But the Saints were his real love, the one place where he could not only pop the popcorn, but where he could decide which movies to show when, to use his favorite analogy. Once Goldklang took control of the team he immediately immersed himself—by himself—in the task of procuring talent for his new club. Goldklang is as gentle and generous a wealthy person as there is, but when he wants something he is tenacious, and his preoccupation with fielding an outstanding baseball team in the Northern League paid off with easily the most talented club in the circuit. His wife, Sheila, spent many plane rides with her husband when he had his nose sunk into the latest issue of *Baseball America*, seeing who had been released, who was playing well and who was not. With the combination of rookies and veterans Goldklang was able to piece together by virtue of major-league organizations' mistakes and oversights, there was no reason for the Saints not to be the class of the league.

And true to expectations, the St. Paul Saints were rarely outplayed. They invariably hit better than their opponents, and they usually pitched better as well. But there were slips: pitches thrown without proper forethought—3-1 fastballs down the middle of the plate are just asking to be taken out of the yard—a booted ground ball here, a pickoff throw put in the first-base dugout there, all mixed in with a team putting too much pressure on itself to lead the Northern League from opening day through the final game. The losses are bound to come. Blackwell and Eppard were perfectly willing to accept defeat, as long as their opponents actually beat them. When the Saints brought defeat upon themselves, there was nothing to do but get the players to relax a little and focus more on playing a game, not studying the standings and statistics.

As this conversation was going on, Grundy the bus driver was looking more and more perplexed, with his chubby legs hugging the steering wheel and his arms draped over it. At the spot in Iowa where Highway 70 forks north and west, he was faced with the two ultimate bus-driver dilemmas: Which way do I go? and, Should I let everybody know I'm lost?

The second one was easy. Grundy got lost all the time, so much so that it was almost taken for granted. On the team's second trip to Duluth, he rambled right past the freeway exit for the hotel, even though he had been there three weeks before, and the building and its twenty five-foot sign were clearly visible from the highway. As for the first question, checking a map, apparently, was out of the question, so Grundy had no clue. Maybe somebody else might know.

"Do we go right here, or straight?" he called out behind him. Eppard and Blackwell and Fricke—all veterans of years of minor-league bus trips—looked at one another in confounded disbelief. Players, lacking any rational response to a bus driver who didn't know how to get where he was going, just started laughing. "Don't be asking us," Blackwell told him. "You're the one who's supposed to know." By the time they got everything figured out (Grundy had gone straight at the fork), the bus was heading in the right direction anyway. As the bus hit the outer limits of Sioux City, Iowa, Grundy leaned back again.

"You guys know where the ballpark is?"

"No," Blackwell replied, "and we're going to the hotel first, anyway."

"OK, where's the hotel?"

Two rows back, 6-foot-7 Jim Manfred, who somehow had managed to find a comfortable position to sleep, looked up from his pillow. "Good thing we find these things out before we take off."

Finally, at the outskirts of Sioux City, amid stockyards and factories, a good eight miles on the other side of town from the Holiday Inn, Grundy stopped at a gas station and Fricke went bounding in. If you want something done right, let the trainer do it, or so goes the baseball adage. So Fricke, who carried the unofficial title of traveling secretary along with his real job of tending to the Saints players' aches and pains, finally got the team to the hotel.

On minor-league teams with major-league affiliations, and even on some independent clubs, management imposes pool rules. On some clubs that means you can't lounge by the pool at all; on others there is a pool curfew, often one p.m. on a typical day with a 4:00 or 4:15 bus to the ballpark for a 7:05 game. If players spend too much time relaxing under the hot sun, the thinking goes, their brains will curdle, their throwing arms will turn to mush, and their feet will shrink and slip out of their spikes on an important play where they need to make a diving catch. Or something like that. Tim Blackwell had been a part of too many of those organizations, and he had had to deal with too many of those rules. He was released as manager of the New York Mets' Columbia, South Carolina, club in the Single A South Atlantic League after two consecutive championship seasons, in part because the home office felt he was too soft on his players, whether they won three-fifths of their ballgames or not. So now that he was running the show, Blackwell was going to see to it that his players enjoyed themselves, even if that meant baking themselves by the pool. He might even join them.

July 6 was a simmering, blindingly bright Tuesday when Kevin Millar pulled up a chaise lounge, stripped to his shorts and began the process of toasting his skin to a crisp golden brown. Blackwell did indeed join him, while his twin boys chased each other around the pool in their pre-swim ritual. A native of San Diego, Blackie had a Californian's affinity for the sun, and he was not about to let some free time slip by without catching some rays. He and Kevin began talking about the team and its fortunes, now that Thunder Bay had slipped past the Saints into first place, on the strength of seven straight wins at home. The wire-to-wire dream was dead, and for the eternal optimist Tim Blackwell, that was for the best.

"See," he explained as both he and Millar faced skyward, Tim's palms gesturing towards the clouds even when he was prone, their eyes shut against the blazing sun, "now the pressure is off to lead wire-to-wire, and we can just settle down and relax, and play baseball. Until now, everybody was trying so hard, thinking they had to play perfect baseball and win every game—nobody can do that. When you push like that, you start making dumb decisions." Blackwell recalled a play the day before in which Eppard, an eleven-year veteran and probably the king of fundamental baseball, took a ground ball at first and had a play on a runner heading for third. Instead of setting and making a strong throw, Eppard threw off balance as quickly as he could, putting the ball past Greg D'Alexander into the stands and sending the runner home. "That play at third, with Jim Eppard, the best, most steady player you'd ever want, thought he had to rush the throw when he had plenty of time, and he wound up short-arming it and throwing it away. He knows better than that, and he knew it right away. Everybody is trying to kill the ball, and they wind up not hitting anything. Everybody we've faced has pitched slow, but we're trying so hard to kill the ball that nothing happens."

When Tim Blackwell was drafted out of high school in 1970 by the Boston Red Sox, he figured he would give baseball a try, and if it didn't work out, he'd move on to something else. When he was bouncing around the minor leagues and being called up to the majors and sent back down again, he and his wife, Jane, decided that their baseball life would soon be over. When his playing career was winding down in the mid-1980s, he and Jane agreed that maybe it was about time to try something else. But in the spring of 1993, with his options in organized baseball exhausted for that year, Blackwell accepted an unlikely offer from an investment banker who owned an offbeat team in an improbable league. It was like Blackwell said on the first day of practice back in June: "This is year number twenty-four in professional baseball, and I've got three pink slips and I've been fired two other times. And I'm still kicking, and. I'm still fighting, and I think there's a lot of fight left. They're going to have to tear this stuff off of me, or bury me in it. I can't help it. I enjoy being out here."

It took a lot longer in year number twenty-four than in year number one for Blackwell to explain why he was still there. Now everything he did involved not only Jane, but fifteen-year-old Jana, thirteen-year-old Jamie, and twins Michael and Matthew, who had seen more cities and more baseball stadiums and more ballplayers in their nine years than most people see in a lifetime. Blackwell was convinced that one of the reasons the Mets released him after winning two straight South Atlantic League championships was because he was expensive. He always had it written into his contract that the club had to pay not only for him to move to the town he would be managing in, but his entire family as well.

Tim Blackwell is a remarkable piece of work on the field. After years living as a backup catcher—in a decade as a major-league catcher with the Red Sox, Cubs, Phillies, and Expos, he played in more than a hundred games in a season only once—Blackwell learned to sit next to coaches. It could be the manager, the hitting coach, the pitching coach, but whoever it was, he always listened. He learned which pitches to call for what hitters in any situation. He picked up what pitch to look for at the plate, depending on the count or on which bases are runners. He knew which fielders should play where for which hitters, and when which baserunners should run when and how far. He had the fundamentals down, and as a manager he dispatched them with a calmness under fire that never cracked, no matter how poorly the team was playing. He knew it, and that was not the part of baseball that, almost halfway through the season, was beginning to run streaks of gray through his brown hair and bushy mustache. "On the field, between the lines, it's a piece of cake. It's the moving, supporting a family, that's hard. Still, you do it because you enjoy all the different things that are involved. You certainly don't do it for the fame and notoriety, because who cares?"

Those are the words of a spiritual, deeply religious man. And don't think for a minute that it's easy to keep one's faith in a baseball locker room, where the language and morals are the antithesis of anything you'd hear in any church on Sunday. Tim and Jane Blackwell discovered their faith in 1973, when he was playing in Bristol, Connecticut, for the Red Sox Double A team in the Eastern League. They've developed their beliefs since then, taking their children out of public school and teaching them at home, with a Christian curriculum that reflected their credences. But Blackwell was not a part of any God squad, as he called it; it would surprise many on his team that he was so totally religious. Blackwell laughed and kidded and played practical jokes at least as much and as well as anybody else on the St. Paul Saints. When the Saints were making a flurry of roster moves towards the end of July, Blackwell called Kevin Millar into his glass-walled office in the clubhouse and closed the door, at a time when Millar was the hottest star on the team. Things weren't going well with the Saints on the field, Blackwell told Millar. The team wasn't winning, and the cohesion that had propelled the club into first place early on was gone. It was time to make a change. Millar's eyes opened wide, and his jaw dropped at the thought that he could be released after playing so well.

"You'll be hitting earlier in the batting order," Blackwell told Millar, as his teammates erupted in laughter just outside Blackwell's office.

Indeed, Blackie had no desire to force his beliefs on his players. "I've been called to do something that I know something about," he explained. "If in any way, shape, or form my actions can help somebody out and point them in

a positive direction, then I think I'm doing what I'm supposed to be doing. I'm not going to shove my beliefs and
feelings down other people's throats. At the same time, if I
stand up for what I believe in, I'm exposing myself."

Believe it or not, that's what got Blackwell into trouble.
Over the years, after watching managers and coaches that
nurtured, supported, and helped their charges become
better players and people, and others who tried to scream
and intimidate their way to winning seasons, Blackwell discovered something: baseball is a game. You're supposed to
have fun at it. It's a lesson that's sometimes difficult even
for Blackwell to remember, what with being fired and all,
for the transgression of not being stern enough with his
players, and wondering whether his last games with the
Columbia Mets of the Single A South Atlantic League were
his last in organized baseball, but it was central enough to
his philosophy of the game—and of life—that he managed
to keep it in mind. "I've always told myself that if I ever
crossed that line into coaching—whether it was high school,
college, or the pros—I was going to make sure the guys who
played for me were going to learn, number one, to play the
game, but also to enjoy themselves. Because if you don't
enjoy yourself in this game, you might as well not be out
there. The easiest thing in the world is to get out of bed in
the morning and know you are going to be in the lineup.
That's a piece of cake. The guys who have the hardest time
are the guys who play once a week and they don't know
when they're going to play."

After a while, Blackie mentions the other reason he
keeps coming back in an effort to make it to the big
leagues. Under the terms of the contract between Major
League Baseball and its players, Blackwell officially has
seven and a half years of big-league experience. To become
fully vested in the major-league pension, he needs ten
years. It's not a trivial landmark, either. Blackwell was never
a superstar, and he only played at the very beginning of the
baseball salary explosion, so he never reaped the benefits
many of baseball's even mediocre players do now. But to get
the full major-league pension in 1993, when Blackwell was

managing the Saints, was to cash checks of more than $70,000 a year, a figure that increased every year. Blackwell wanted the satisfaction of showing he could coach in the majors, but he also wanted the security it would bring for his family.

But a funny thing happened on the way back to the show. After having to be coaxed into taking a questionable managing job with a new team in an upstart league, Tim Blackwell fell in love with independent baseball. His sons traveled with him on the road. His daughters worked in the Saints' office. His wife came to the games early and stayed late, chatting with everybody from Marv Goldklang to Mike Veeck's toddler daughter, Rebecca. Blackwell quickly learned this was not the corporate vanilla brand of baseball Americans had subsisted on for too long. This was a game that people could come and enjoy, just as he tried to teach that same love of the sport to his players. He wanted the pension, and he wanted the satisfaction of showing he could compete at the game's top levels. But after he was done, Blackwell wanted to come back to independent baseball. "I would like to coach third base for somebody, get two and a half years and max out on my pension, really get out of debt," He confessed. "Then I'd love to come back and do this same thing, independent baseball, until they bury me into the ground."

The movie "Field of Dreams" has become part of baseball folklore in the years since it came out. Kevin Costner heard the voices imploring, "If you build it, they will come," and he plowed a baseball diamond out of his Iowa cornfield in search of the dreams he thought he would never be able to pursue. The parallels to the new park in Sioux City, Iowa, were creepy.

A couple miles past the edge of the 100,000-person city's inhabited points, you come to Line Drive, a new road built specifically for Lewis and Clark Park, home of the Sioux City Explorers. Only the buffer of a newly paved parking lot separates the shiny new bleachers and still unstained concrete from a hundred acres of towering cornstalks. If you've seen the movie, you half expect Shoeless Joe Jackson to materialize from amongst the husks and bring his friends from the 1919 Chicago White Sox to play a ballgame. In fact, if not for the freeway atop the rising knoll beyond center field, an Explorers fan might never have any idea he or she were in the vicinity of a populated area, and not in the middle of nowhere. It might as well be.

But the stadium itself was civilization personified. The town fathers put out bids and asked how much it would cost to put up the finest, most modern, state-of-the-art baseball stadium, with every amenity of the best major-league parks, on a minor-league scale with 3,800 seats. Four million smackers, was the reply. Build it, said the Sioux City honchos. They'll come.

Those folks in Iowa clearly knew what they were talking about. After buying their computer-printed tickets, fans walked in and saw plenty of gleaming concession stands, a souvenir counter, even a fully-stocked bar, arrayed before them. Once they ascended the steps (or took the elevator) and reached their seats—these were molded plastic, theater-style seats, of course—they saw a brand new, carefully graded and meticulously kept field, reigned in by a twelve-foot high wall that was far enough away from home plate to make hitters actually have to work for a home run. This park was legit. If the fans in the box seats or the reporters in the press box were hungry, they need only flag down a waitress and place their order; it would be cheerfully delivered within an inning. Of course, the wait staff also serviced the four skyboxes, though they didn't need to bring drinks. The luxury boxes all had wet bars.

CHAPTER SIX

Hitting Optional

Doubleheaders in minor-league baseball—held almost exclusively to make up rainouts—generally consist of two, seven-inning games. On July 9 in Duluth, seven innings apiece was all the St. Paul Saints could handle, and it was all Jim Manfred could stomach.

Manfred, a thin, blonde pitcher who talked like the Minnesota native he was—the 6-foot-7 player who stood to lose the most from Duluth's perilous dugout with its low clearances—walked into Wade Stadium with the league's best earned run average, 2.16 runs allowed per nine innings pitched. In the baseball business, stats like that are impressive, especially from a starter like Manfred, who pitched longer than relievers and had more opportunities to let in runs. Yet his won-lost record stood at 0-2. How does someone lead a league in pitching, yet not win a game? Manny had struck out twice as many batters as he had walked, he had given up fewer than one hit an inning, he had started six games, had gone the distance once, had thrown more than thirty-three innings, and had permitted only eight earned runs—and he still had not won a game. Maybe Manfred should have come up with some excuse to stay home for this Duluth trip. As bad as his luck had been through the season, it would get worse.

He started the first game of the doubleheader against the Dukes, which was being held to make up for the rainout during the season's opening series. His form was superb, his pitch selection was excellent, and his fastball speed approaching ninety miles an hour. Everything was working.

Indeed, after allowing two hits in the first inning, Manfred was virtually untouchable through the remaining six. He struck out the side in order in the second inning, and only one other runner got past second base. That runner happened to score, the result of an error, an unearned run. A brilliant game.

But Todd LeValley, Duluth's unremarkable right-hander, was having a brilliant game of his own. If Tommy Raffo didn't exist, he would have had a no-hitter. Raffo singled and doubled; the rest of the Saints' hitters did absolutely nothing. In the course of his two-hitter, LeValley walked exactly one batter, and despite his three base runners he faced only one batter above the minimum, thanks to a fortuitous pickoff play and an ill-advised attempt by Raffo to steal second base. Once again Manfred pitched—not just threw, but pitched—a sparkling game, only to see himself and the team lose another game because the bats didn't produce. A younger, less mature Manfred might have kicked things and scowled. But this Manfred complimented his teammates on a good game and went into the clubhouse by himself to shower and think.

He returned from the clubhouse in the middle of the second inning of the second game, only to see that his teammates had put five runs on the board in the first eight batters for Ranbir Grewal, who had started the second game. Leon Durham had hit a three-run homer, Keith Gogos had hit one of the most thundering shots in Wade Stadium history, a blast that would have gone more than 450 feet if the Dukes hadn't thought to extend a net forty feet above the left-field wall to catch such projectiles, and Jerry DeFabbia had doubled and scored on Kevin Millar's single. Manfred surveyed the scene, looked at the runs that could have—should have—been his, and with all his power kicked the plastic garbage can holding the bats. "Oh, now you all decide to score some runs!"

Then Manfred laughed. He was only kidding.

Jim Manfred, after all, was happy to still be playing baseball, and to be doing it so close to home.

By the time he signed a contract with the St. Paul Saints at age twenty-four, Manfred had already been cut in high school, in junior college, and by the New York Mets. His baseball career had gotten off to a terrible start—his high school coach in Bloomington, a Minneapolis suburb, didn't like Manfred and wouldn't keep him on the team. He wound up playing high school hockey, eventually ending up with the St. Paul Vulcans, a semi-professional junior-league club. But still he wanted to pitch, so he tried out at Normandale Community College in the Twin Cities. The coach there called Manfred's high school coach to find out why such a seemingly impressive talent had ridden the bench and then had left the team. He was told that Manfred had an attitude problem and was more trouble than he was worth. That was the end of Manfred's brief run at Normandale. He finally wound up at tiny Indian Hills Community College in Iowa, where he pitched nearly every day and caught the attention of the Mets, who drafted him in the thirty-fifth round of the 1990 draft.

Manfred floundered after he was drafted, partly because he started playing professional ball in June, immediately after a long college season, and partly because he was assigned to Sarasota in the Rookie Gulf Coast League in southwest Florida. Games there start at ten in the morning, and by the time the contest is over, the temperature is usually edging close to a hundred degrees. And if it's the humidity that gets you and not the heat, then southwest Florida at high noon in July is a killer for a pitcher standing exposed to the baking sun on the mound. Manfred struggled to a 1-3 record with three saves and a 3.18 ERA, but after a winter of rest the Mets moved him up to Pittsfield in the short-season Single A New York-Penn League, and he started to show the promise that everybody knew was there.

He began the year as Pittsfield's closer, going 6-0 with four saves. He went more than twenty innings at one point without giving up a run, and his overall ERA was 0.02. Then he felt a twinge in his right shoulder, but Manfred was determined to ignore it and continue on his roll. The twinge quickly evolved into full-blown pain, which developed into sharp anguish, to the point where he could barely lift his arm. It was a torn rotator cuff, the injury pitchers dread to face, and before the season was over Manfred's record stood at 6-4, his ERA of 4.18, and he still had those same four saves. Team trainers prescribed rest, and the Mets decided to give Manfred another shot one rung up the ladder, at full-season Single A Columbia of the South Atlantic League, with manager Tim Blackwell.

Blackwell and his staff tried everything they could think of to help Manfred work through his injury, from rest to extra exercise and conditioning, but none of it worked. Manfred's shoulder was getting worse, and to keep the pain from becoming unbearable he was changing his pitching motion. The injury didn't hurt as much, but his pitches were not nearly as effective either. Manny finished the year at 3-4 with a 3.54 ERA, and the Mets decided to send him to New York for surgery.

"I thought I was done," he remembered. "I was scared to death. I had to fly into LaGuardia by myself, with nobody there to meet me, so I called a cab and had the cab ride from hell. I thought this cab was going to fall apart before we got there, and this guy was shooting in and out of traffic so much I was sure he was going to kill us. At the hospital, I almost had them talked out of doing it. I thought it would be a check against me for the Mets. But they did it anyway, and with the arthroscope I watched the whole thing on TV. I couldn't believe it was my arm there on the screen."

The operation was a success, and the Mets took care of Manfred's physical therapy in Minnesota during the off-season. He came back to spring training in 1993 with new optimism and a Triple A contract. He didn't want to blow his arm out in camp, so he started throwing gradually, not going all-out at first, and no coach told him to do otherwise. Then at 7:30 on the last morning of spring training, as his parents were flying in from Minneapolis to watch their son play baseball, Manfred was called into the minor-league office and told that after three innings of work during the entire spring, his fastball was not where the club thought it should be. He was released.

"The first thing I felt was that I couldn't believe it. It was like somebody telling you your dog died or your dad died. It was like, what do I do now? I wanted to jump over the table and wring the guy's neck. One day I was on the field with Bobby Bonilla and Eddie Murray, hitting ground balls and playing catch. The next day I was gone. I couldn't believe it." So Manfred gathered up his things from his locker, packed his suitcase, and caught a plane home, crossing paths with his parents, who never did get to see their son play for the Mets.

It was too late in the spring for Manny to latch on with another organization, so he decided to head back to Bloomington and get back to work on his successful landscaping business. His fiancé was pregnant with their first child, and he had given baseball a chance, no matter how frustrating his run had been. Then Marv Goldklang called, explained the Northern League to Manfred, and asked if he might be interested in pitching for the Saints. Manfred said no. Goldklang persisted. He kept calling back. After all, he said, Manfred could work at his business in the morning, making some real money, and then head for the ballpark in the afternoon. Finally, Manfred relented. He would play.

Manfred may have had lousy luck up to that point as a St. Paul Saint, but he was not the only one. Saints pitchers were increasingly falling victim to their hitters' inability to put the ball in play—and to other Saints pitchers.

John Thoden was a promising pitcher in the Expos organization before he fell victim to the numbers game—a phrase that pops up so much in baseball talk that it has almost becomes a cliche, a catch-all for a team releasing a player for no good reason, simply because there weren't enough spots for him. Thoden pitched in Salt Lake City with the independent Trappers of the rookie Pioneer League, going 9-3 and helping that team win the league championship. He latched on with the Saints, like everyone else, believing he could pitch and determined to prove it. The fierce determination showed, like when his propensity to give up home runs kicked in and he would return to the dugout, compliment his teammates on their fielding, and implore them to pick him up and get him some runs. Then he would walk quietly through the runway into the clubhouse. There would be a reverberating bang of hand striking metal locker, followed by a thundering scream.

There were no gopher balls on July 11, as the Saints tried desperately to salvage what was fast becoming a disastrous four-game series. Following Manfred's anguished loss, Grewal left after the fourth inning with the score tied 5-5. On came Paul Marak, a veteran middle reliever who had spent time with the Atlanta Braves before coming down with arm problems. Trouble was, his arm problems never went away, and Marak was too wary of facing the end of his career to tell anybody this. But everybody knew he was trying to pitch through his pain. His fastball had lost the pop that got him to the major leagues, and his curve didn't snap. Marak would wince after nearly every delivery. The hitters knew what was coming, and they knew they could hit it. Starters began to dread seeing Marak get up to work in the bullpen, lest they see their leads evaporate with a few ill-placed pitches. This time it was thirteen pitches to four batters, all but one of them lazy fastballs, only four of them strikes (two of those strikes were stroked for singles). Two hits, two walks, two runs, and the Saints lost 7-5.

The next day the Saints squeaked by with a win by a similar 7-5 score, and they entered the series finale down two games to one to the last-place Dukes. Now, losing to the cellar-dwellers was bad enough. But losing to Mal Fichman's cellar-dwellers was unconscionable, especially when those losses had helped Mal pull his club up in the standings. A win was imperative.

Fortunately, though, Thoden made the Dukes keep the ball in the park, and he was locked in a scoreless pitchers duel heading into the eighth. The number-eight hitter, Mike Smedes, a rookie in his first week of professional ball, stroked a double. Dana Williams followed with another double, sending Blackwell to the mound and Thoden to the showers to shout expletives with one run in and a man on second with nobody out. Another reason John was shouting was because Marak was coming in.

Sacrifice fly. Intentional walk. Double. Double. Single. Home run. Six batters, four hits, six runs (one of them charged to Thoden). And the Saints never did manage to score.

On the very, very quiet bus heading home from Duluth that night, Blackie didn't say much, except that there would be no batting practice the next day. Maybe not practicing would shake the team out of its hitting slump. "Hitting in the cage is optional tomorrow," Tim said. He thought for a minute and added, "But hitting during the game is not optional."

Stephane Dionne had a question. Another question. Seems Stephane was always asking questions, always wanting to know things he did not, and to get clarifications on things he thought he knew, lest he be mistaken. He came to St. Paul from Rimouski, Quebec, a distant outpost two hundred miles northeast of Quebec City, a hockey town in a hockey province in a hockey country, where even if the population was mad about baseball, they would only have a couple of months to play before the cold and snow would force them to put away the bats and balls and break out the skates and pucks. He grew up speaking French, only really learning enough English to get by when he started commuting to Florida in an annual pilgrimage in search of a professional baseball job.

His teammates were forever dogging him (a term, meaning to kid somebody, whose meaning Dionne learned only after the first time he took some ribbing too seriously and someone had to tell him, "We're just dogging you, Stephane"). His English was still getting better, and now he could keep up with virtually any conversation, but he often felt he had to repeat things to make sure he got it right. "Hey, Stephane, you want to play pepper?" "Pepper?" After a while, the team bus was a cacophony of ballplayers repeating everything anyone said, and laughing. "Stryker, did you fart?" "Fart?"

His question this time was about colleges. Dionne had gone to college in Canada, earning a degree. But a Canadian college is the equivalent of a U.S. technical college; a university is where Canadians go to earn four-year degrees. But universities are expensive, and Stephane did not have very much money when he was growing up. Besides, Canada does not have many college baseball teams, and baseball was the bottom line for Stephane Dionne. Still, there was the question.

"What do you know about the University of Oklahoma?" What do you want to know? It's a pretty good school, it's big, what else? "What about the baseball team?" You mean the one that perennially makes it to the College World Series, the national power that seems guaranteed by birthright a spot in the Top-twenty-five rankings for eternity? It's fine. "Oh, well, Keith Lyttle, the Duluth hitting coach, is a coach there. He just offered me a scholarship there."

To say this was a piece of fortuitous news for Dionne would be an understatement similar to calling Babe Ruth a slap singles hitter. Of course, as the afternoon wore on, the facts were only slightly less remarkable than Stephane's telling of them—not because he intentionally misled anyone, but because he was talking about a university in Oklahoma, so why not just call it the University of Oklahoma. He came back shortly afterward and announced it was actually Oklahoma State University, still a fine school and a national baseball power. Later, it turned out it was Oklahoma City University, a private college with 8,000 students and a fine reputation, not to mention a very good (but much lower level) baseball program.

No matter. This was an appropriate end to a run of persistence and mettle that defined Stephane Dionne as someone who ought always to be reckoned with, if only because he simply will not give up.

Stephane's dream—that's what he called it, his dream —began in Rimouski, when as a young teenager he saw the Montreal Expos on television, and he watched with wonder the play of catcher Gary Carter, the Expos' superstar-in-residence. That was it. All his friends wanted to be Guy LaFleur and play hockey for the Montreal Canadiens, but Dionne wanted to be Gary Carter and catch for the Montreal Expos. Youth baseball in Rimouski was not exactly all the rage, especially since prime baseball weather lasted only about two months in this frigid climate. So Stephane learned how to play baseball by watching Carter play on TV and mimicking his catching style, his swing, his mannerisms. But snippets of televised games do not a baseball education make, and Stephane did not start out as a very good baseball player. When he tried out for his first team as a Rimouski teenager, he did not make it, and he thought about giving up. But his father, Lorenzo, intoned his oft-repeated admonition that his son would not succeed at anything, including baseball, if he did not practice and keep working until he got it right. Certainly Lorenzo hoped Stephane would take his advice, but even he could not have imagined the lengths to which his son would go to follow through on making his baseball dream reality.

When he began to show serious promise as a left-handed hitting catcher at age sixteen, Dionne decided to move two hundred miles to the southwest, to Quebec City, where he could participate in strong youth leagues and face the good pitching that would make him better. He went to school there and lived by himself in a rooming house while he spent his days studying and playing, and doing little else. Stephane did well there, but few scouts make their way to the eastern reaches of French Canada, so he had to begin making his opportunities happen by himself. His first break came because he spoke French (it would probably be his last baseball break because of his first language). He received an offer to play for a team in Bordeaux for the French professional league: room, board, use of a car, $250 a week, and the opportunity to travel around France for a summer. In return, Stephane was a player-coach, teaching the game to others in French. It was great fun, but for a would-be pro baseball player it was like losing a summer. If few scouts get to Quebec City, none make their way to France, unless they're on vacation, in which case a baseball game is the last thing they want to see. The competition was weak, and Dionne's baseball skills advanced little that summer.

Then he decided, if he wanted to get the attention of baseball teams, he ought to go to where the baseball teams are. So Stephane Dionne went to Florida. He received an offer to play in a new, Florida-based winter league, with former major leaguer Bobby Bonds as commissioner. It would be Stephane's first opportunity to show his worth, against real competition, to major-league scouts. As he would say, it would be his big chance to achieve his dream. But the league folded before its first pitch was thrown. Some of the investors got the jitters and pulled out their money, and Dionne was left in a strange place with no money, no job, and increasingly little hope. He had to make a decision: either he had to go home, get a job, devote himself to his girl-friend, Annick, and give up the dream; or he could stick around and give the dream another chance.

So Stephane did the Stephane thing. He stuck around until the winter meetings, sleeping in his tiny red subcompact car and getting a job setting tables at a Miami seaside hotel. He waited until the winter meetings there, and hounded scouts until one from the New York Yankees agreed to watch him play the next day. Dionne played well, and the scout told him to go back to Canada, and he would work to get him a spot in the Yankees' spring training camp. Stephane was back in Rimouski in time for Christmas 1991, thinking his dream would soon become reality. But the Yankees offer fell through. The scout called Stephane and explained that though he had recommended him highly to team management, the Yankees were reluctant to offer a valuable spring-training slot to someone with no statistics in any league the club knew anything about. They had no yardstick to measure him by, so they weren't going to measure him at all. But the scout gave Dionne the phone number of Nick Belmonte, who was then the manager of the Salt Lake City Trappers, an independent team in the Pioneer League.

Stephane called Belmonte, who invited him to a Trappers tryout camp in Florida that March. It was back to Florida again, where Stephane sought out his baseball deity, Gary Carter, who was preparing for spring training himself. Ask Stephane, and he would be happy to haul out his collection of photos of Gary Carter and Stephane Dionne, smiling broadly, each with an arm draped over the other's shoulder. During their meeting, Dionne also managed to slip in a request for Carter to call Belmonte and recommend him as a hard-working go-getter, a good kid who deserved a chance. Carter said he would, but Stephane figured he was just being nice.

He wasn't. As Belmonte tells the story, Dionne had told him of his adoration of Carter, and how he had asked Carter to give him a reference. Nick had filed it away and forgotten about it. "Then the phone rang one day, I picked it up, and damn if it isn't Gary Carter." He told Belmonte that he had never seen Stephane play, but he seemed like someone who at least deserved a look.

Belmonte gave Dionne a look, and he liked the twenty-two-year-old Canadian enough to ask him to come to Chicago a couple of months later, when the Trappers would be holding another camp. Stephane agreed to show up there, heading first to Guelph, Ontario, to keep his skills sharp by playing on a semipro team there. But a California Angels scout happened to see Stephane belt a home run for Guelph in the interim, and he told Dionne that some other Angels scouts would be by soon and he wanted them to take a look as well. They were supposed to be there the same day as the Trappers' Chicago tryout. Stephane called Belmonte, explaining that he had to choose between his shot with the Trappers and with the Angels. Belmonte told him to stay there and see the Angels scouts. If he had the chance to sign with a major-league organization, Nick told him, that should easily take precedence over an independent team. The Angels scouts gave Stephane another look, took down his phone number, and said they were interested in signing him. But they never did. Dionne's life was beginning to form a familiar, disheartening pattern.

The next winter, in late 1992, it was back to Belmonte, who had become the scouting director for the Northern League. He told Stephane about the league, and about its tryouts in Florida the following February. Stephane made the trek again, and slept in his car again, all for the chance to be seen. He went to the Ft. Myers camp, and performed well. But there were still other camps to be held, and the teams were not ready to sign anybody yet. Then a Houston Astros scout saw Stephane play and invited him to the Astros' spring training. With every setback, it seemed, Stephane still managed to inch one step closer to that elusive dream.

But at least this time he was wearing the uniform of a major-league baseball organization, staying in a dormitory with other baseball players, having someone else pay for his meals, and he had the privilege of playing baseball. That privilege lasted two weeks, until the team needed to decide whether to stick with its bonus babies and the players it had already decided were marked to do well in the Astros organization. For Stephane, it was back to his tiny car, his home away from Rimouski, and back to another Northern League camp, this one in Pompano Beach, Florida.

The pattern remained the same. Again, Dionne put forth an impressive performance, and again he received plenty of encouraging words but no contract. He spoke at length with Marv Goldklang and Tim Blackwell, who were very nice, but they did not have pens or legal documents in their hands. "I was confused," Stephane remembered about his baseball odyssey. "I did so many things, I proved again and again I could play—I proved it to everybody else, and I proved it to myself. What the hell else could I do?"

He was on the verge once again of giving up the dream, of returning to Rimouski and living a normal, baseball-free life, when Belmonte suggested he give it one more shot and show up for the last Northern League camp, in St. Paul at the beginning of June. Stephane didn't know what to think or what to do, but before he could ponder the alternatives, his mouth had already said yes, and he was back in his car, this time headed for Minnesota.

The final Northern League camp was dangerously close to a joke. All the clubs had signed most of their players already, but the Saints had placed a newspaper ad anyway, exhorting anybody and everybody who had a mitt and a pair of spikes to come out for their big shot to become a professional ballplayer. The field was packed with 150 players, some overweight, some who hadn't swung at a ball in years, some whose athletic experience consisted of nothing more than Wednesday night softball games where the most important consideration is that someone remembered to stock the beer cooler. That was the bad news. The good news was that Stephane stood out as one of only a small handful of people who could actually play. The only other catcher in the camp dropped out after the first day, so Stephane caught for more than five hours, then stood in at the plate and belted a home run. Thunder Bay manager Dan Schwam saw this, but he wasn't interested. Neither was anybody else. Tim Blackwell saw Dionne, shook his hand, and said he was sorry, but the team already had enough catchers. It was, Stephane remembered, "the worst day of my life."

Things got better, though. Goldklang and Blackwell finally offered Dionne the bullpen catcher's spot, meaning he wasn't on the roster and couldn't play in games, but he would get paid and he got to wear the uniform. It was only a tenuous thread on the hem of his baseball dream, but once again, it was a little closer than where he was before. He took it. And though he did not enjoy the status of being only a bullpen catcher, for Stephane it was just another unexpected turn on his road to his nirvana: his signature on a professional baseball contract. "I picked the toughest way to make it. I came to them, they didn't come to me. What else can I do? I've done everything I can think of. It still hurts inside, but anytime I'm on a baseball field, I'm happy."

CHAPTER SEVEN

Pigs, Polkas, and the Other Trappings of Baseball

For all his bravado and shows of irreverence, Mike Veeck is a very calculating and cautious man at heart. His job as president and one-third owner of the St. Paul Saints was to put rear ends on the seats, and part of how he did that was to create the personality and the atmosphere he thought would be conducive to that. It worked.

So when the Saints' staff sat down before the season began and tried figure out what time of day to start the games, and when Dave Wright, the media relations director and a mainstay in the local sports scene for years, suggested several noon games during the week, Veeck balked. That would be a risk, he said, a gamble not worth taking. He might have been outrageous, but Veeck didn't want to do anything that would screw up his team's revenue potential. Offering what, in less enlightened days, would have been called a businessman's special was fine for major-league teams like the Twins, who could draw 15,000 or 20,000 just by opening the gates and breaking out the cash box. Such games give those clubs an opportunity to draw in a whole different clientele. But for a fledgling team like the St. Paul Saints—a club, at the time, that no one could guarantee would succeed—Veeck thought the club needed to nurture the ticket buyers it already had. He thought having games at noon, when many loyal Saints fans couldn't attend, might turn off just enough people to turn the team's balance sheet red. Finally, though, he agreed to experiment with one early game. July 13 would be the day.

Imagine Veeck's surprise, then, when 4,746 people—ninety-four percent of capacity—turned out for that noon game, despite dingy, low, unwelcoming clouds, a steady mist and temperatures that never approached seventy. In his uncertainty, though, Mike Veeck had been certain he needed something to keep fans entertained. He found Jerry Jeff Walker, in town for a concert that night, a mainstay of the country-blues-folk-rock set, a man who had seen a lot in his years in the music business, who had made a few bucks off his hit, "Mr. Bojangles," but who had never thrown out the first pitch at a baseball game—in the eighth inning.

It's true. The king of the gimmick had again come up with one no one had ever heard of, throwing out the first pitch after the real pitchers had thrown about two hundred real pitches. But after the visitor's half of the eighth, on came Stephane Dionne—whose name Al Frechtman called over the PA system, more recognition that Dionne usually gets this late in a game—to crouch behind the plate and catch Walker's lob from the pitcher's mound. Stephane and Jerry Jeff shook hands, the singer asked the catcher to autograph the ball, and he was on his way. This was Stephane, of course, so he didn't have a clue who this guy was. He just did what he was asked and went back to the bullpen. After the game, he asked, "Who was that guy?" When he found out who, Stephane (being Stephane, the man who went through the season hardly ever paying for a meal, and who even finagled a free limo to pick up his girl-friend at the airport and a free oil change for his car) made a few calls and got into Walker's concert for free, and had a few beers backstage with the musician and his band.

Anybody who spent time at a few Saints games should not have been surprised that Mike Veeck and his crew would try something as goofy as a late-inning first pitch. By his standards, in fact, it was a little tame. The atmosphere at a St. Paul Saints game ranges somewhere between eccentric and manic. Purists might have balked, had it not been for the fact that this was a place in the Twin Cities to watch professional baseball outdoors, and if not for the knowledge that baseball has a long and important tradition as a bastion for the offbeat—a trail blazed by Mike Veeck's dad. Besides, this was more fun than most people could ever remember having at a baseball game.

July 14 was Bastille Day, and what better way to celebrate than for Frechtman to have Dionne tape record the names and positions of all the players on both teams, as well as all his between-inning announcements, in French, so Frechtman could conduct a bilingual baseball game. It was the way Al Frechtman worked. An actor with a background in comedy, and a former member of Garrison Keillor's entourage on the nationally-broadcast public radio program, "A Prairie Home Companion," as well as a former New York City department-store window dresser, Frechtman did not fit the normal profile of a baseball PA announcer, and his act showed it. As a tape of a French singer crooning Bob Dylan's "The Times They Are A-Changin" that Al had dredged up wafted over the Municipal Stadium loudspeakers, Veeck looked up at the press box and smiled. "You know," he said, "sometime the league ought to fine me for him, just on principle. Marv had the best line: 'What qualifies a window dresser from Brooklyn to be a PA announcer?' Marv, I don't know, and it doesn't really much matter."

It was the way of the Saints.

When the team began the task of interviewing candidates for public-address announcer, it got applicants who had experience as high school, small college, even major college and professional announcers. Jobs were scarce for paid public-address people in the Twin Cities, or anywhere, so this quickly became a plum job. Then along came this comedic actor, about five-foot-six, with long, thinning brown hair and a scraggly beard, with his ever-so-slight Brooklyn intonation, who had never called an inning of a baseball game (though he had seen plenty as a fan), promising to be irreverent and funny. He got the job.

Frechtman came through on that promise. Granted, he had good material to work with, but he delivered it well, and he threw in plenty of ad-libs. It was one thing for ordinary fans to queue up behind the Lovely Gina's barber chair overlooking home plate to get their ten-dollar haircuts while watching the game. It was, after all, Mike Veeck's signature bit, the one stunt he brought with him from Florida. It was another thing altogether for Al Frechtman to string a microphone from the press box and to call an inning while getting a trim, but that's what he did. No shave, though.

At every ballpark, fans sing "Take Me Out to the Ballgame" during the seventh-inning stretch. In a game steeped in tradition, there is none more sacred. Even if fans don't need to, they stand up. Even if they can't carry a tune, they sing. But how many of them know that they are only singing the chorus? Who knows that this song begins:

Kelly, Kelly loves baseball games,
Knows the players, knows all their names ...

If you went to St. Paul Saints games, you knew, because Frechtman played the whole thing. When the song got to "Buy me some peanuts and Cracker Jack," he and the rest of the press-box crew—intern Jessica Jensen, media relations director Dave Wright, radio announcer Doug McLeod, the visiting radio crews, reporters, anybody who could squeeze themselves into the tiny booth—would throw bags of peanuts, Cracker Jack, sunflower seeds, or whatever else they could grab from the concession stands to the fans below, all of whom were screaming and waving their arms wildly to the press box.

Frechtman even made cult heroes out of some Saints players, just by the way he said their names as they came to the plate. Eddie Ortega is one. Already a talented second baseman with plenty of flash, Ortega gained newfound notoriety through Frechtman's telling of his plate appearances: "Now batting, the second baseman, Eddie ORTEEEEEEEEEEEEEEEEEGA!" Frechtman delivered the last name in a hoarse growl that took all the energy he could muster. By the time the season was one-third old, the entire crowd would join Frechtman in screaming Ortega's name. In the final third of the season, Frechtman almost never said Ortega's full name at all. He'd say, "Help me out

here, folks. Now batting, the second baseman, Eddie. . ."
and Ortega's name, lasting five full seconds, would boom
out from more than five thousand diaphragms. Ortega became so popular that Gabe's by the Park—the official Saints
bar—sponsored Eddie Ortega night: when and if Ortega
got a single for his first hit of the night, everybody would
get a free taco at the bar after the game, if he hit a double,
two tacos, and so on. Thankfully for Gabe's bottom line,
Ortega only managed a one-bagger his first time up.

Center fielder Rick Hirtensteiner became another
crowd favorite, partly because of Frechtman's delivery. For
him it was, "Rick HIRT. . .ensteiner," a sharp, staccato first
syllable followed by a pause and then the rest of his name in
a normal voice. Of course, like Ortega, Hirtensteiner was a
good ballplayer, and the fans wouldn't have warmed to him
if he was lousy, but neither would they have written a song
in his honor if there wasn't more to it than that.

That's right, a song. A polka, more precisely. "The
Hirtensteiner Polka." Aficionados of the art form will be
well familiar with "The Lichtensteiner Polka," and a group
of season-ticket holders seated near the press box simply
wrote up their own set of lyrics in homage to their favorite
Saint. If you don't already know the tune, you'll have to use
your imagination, but here are the words anyway:

A hit (stomp-stomp)
We-need-a-hit-right-now-from
Hirtensteiner, Hirtensteiner, Hirtensteiner.
A hit! (stomp-stomp)
We-need-a-hit-right-now-from Hirtensteiner, Hirtensteiner, a hit.
We need a hit from Smith and Blasingame, Ortega, Durham, too.
A hit from Charles and Meadows just to name a few.
But now (stomp-stomp)
We-need-a-hit-right-now-from Hirtensteiner, Hirtensteiner, a hit.
(sit down)

The idea at Municipal Stadium was for there always to be
something happening. If people weren't on the field actually playing baseball, then something else had to be going

on. Fans who were not interested in these other happenings could tune out the other distractions and just concentrate on baseball, but for those who were interested, there was plenty else with which to keep busy. This was, after all, the team that used a pig to carry baseballs to the umpire, and where Sister Rosalind (yes, she was a real nun) and her crew of massage therapists offered half-inning back massages and a view of the action on the field for five bucks. It was where you could get that trim you've been meaning to make an appointment for and not miss a pitch. If baseball was supposed to be fun, Mike Veeck and his crew figured, the entire experience of the baseball game ought to be fun.

To that end, between innings there was some of the traditional minor-league fare, like the bat races where two fans lined up near home plate, bent over, and each placed their heads on the knob of a bat. They each spun around ten times with their foreheads on the bats, then ran (hopefully) in the direction of third base. The first one to touch the base was a winner. Both fans usually wound up looking silly, since spinning around face-down causes one to get very dizzy very quickly, and to have an inclination to veer toward the right. There were races where three fans would push tires around the warning track, a take-off on the dot races so popular on major-league scoreboards. One lucky fan would have the pizza of his or her choice delivered during the sixth or seventh inning or so by a local pizzeria. The owner of the dirtiest car in the parking lot (judged by a member of the Saints staff scouting for grime before the game) received a month of free service from the car wash down the street from the stadium. Then there was the K-Man.

General manager Bill Fanning came up with the idea for the K-Man—picking an opposing player each game to single out; if that batter struck out during the game everybody in attendance won a free bottle of soda from a local convenience store, "K" being the scoring designation for a strike out. But it was Frechtman who made the gag work. In the beginning of the year, he would merely talk up the K-Man, shouting his name and making a big deal of it when he struck out. But after the first eight K-Men of the season had won a two-liter bottle of Coke for every fan (the convenience store couldn't keep this up forever, and later dropped the prize down to a limited selection of twenty-ounce bottles), this promotion became a big deal. Frechtman rose to the occasion.

By the middle of July, when thirty-eight-year-old former National League All-Star Pedro Guerrero—who had latched onto the Sioux Falls Canaries in a last gasp to make it back to the big leagues—was the K-Man, Frechtman had the antic down pat. The first time Guerrero came up to bat, Frechtman simply noted that Pedro was the K-Man, and that if he whiffed everybody there could pick up a twenty-ounce bottle of Mr. Pibb or Mellow Yellow, courtesy of the former St. Louis Cardinal. Guerrero grounded to second. Al mustered the same level of excitement for Pedro's second at-bat, when he grounded out to short. For Guerrero's third trip to the plate, Frechtman implored the crowd to scream at the top of their lungs, wishing for a Pedro strike-out. He ripped a single to left. Now it was time to get serious. When Guerrero headed for home plate in the sixth inning, Frechtman called for the silent treatment. Maybe, if everybody were really quiet, the silence would seep into Guerrero's brain, causing him to lose his concentration and miss badly on strike three. After all, some opposing players had sought out Frechtman before ballgames, asking not to be named the K-Man, saying the distinction gets inside their heads, causing them to lose their focus and to strike out. So for more than a full minute, 5,069 people made barely a sound as Guerrero stood in against Eric Moran, looking at two strikes and a ball before making contact and grounding out once again to the shortstop.

But the game was not over, and Guerrero had not yet made his last trip to the plate. That meant that Frechtman had to reach deep in his reservoir of K-Man gimmicks to figure out a way to get Pedro to strike out. He instructed everybody in the reserved seats behind home plate (where they were protected by the screen) to turn their backs to the field. Everybody else was to stand and place their arms outward in the shape of a "K", willing Guerrero to fail. A little karma can be a powerful thing, apparently. Pedro fouled off Tony Darden's first pitch. He looked at a curve ball for strike two. Darden came next with a slider that tailed away from Guerrero; he swung and missed, and walked back to the dugout clutching his bat and swearing, as the sellout crowd screamed wildly and salivated at the prospect of their free Mr. Pibbs.

Every big league ballpark—and even Sioux City's stadium—has luxury boxes, the plexiglass-encased cocoons where well-heeled baseball fans, or just well-heeled executives who find it is good business to work deals at baseball games, can be hermetically sealed into their own world, watching the game in climate-controlled comfort, and having food and drink brought to them at their whim by waiters. And, of course, if they don't feel like watching the action on the field, they can look upward to the monitor and watch the game on TV, or turn the channel and catch "L.A. Law." Municipal Stadium is many things, lots of them wonderful, but none of them luxurious. But since anything a major-league team can do a Northern League team can do more creatively, the Saints staff came up with its own luxury box, of a fashion. Teaming up with a local futon store, the Saints created in one of the two wells below the raised grandstand that led to the groundskeeper's shed its own luxury box, the Futon Living Room. People whose names were drawn at random at the futon store could lounge around on comfortable futon couches, eating free popcorn and drinking free beer and soda in the well just on the other side of a concrete wall from the visitor's dugout on the first-base side of the field, separated from the game by an eight-foot chain-link gate.

In the other well, this one just to the home plate side of the Saints dugout, was the owner's box. Major-league owner's boxes are usually richly-appointed luxury suites in a choice spot high above the action, but the St. Paul Saints' version was definitely in character. There wasn't much luxury to be had; folks sat on folding chairs, and if somebody happened to bring cookies or cake they rested the box on the golf cart just inside the doorway, and people could pop in and partake. Actually, it wasn't supposed to be a special area for anybody. It just evolved that Marv Goldklang, Bill Murray, Mike Veeck, Bill Fanning, and their families, and league officials like Miles Wolff, Van Schley, Nick Belmonte, and Tom Leip, and their families, and Tim Blackwell's family, needed a good place from which to watch the games, and there were simply no extra seats available for anybody, not even the team owners or the league president. Indeed, when Bill Murray showed up unannounced before one game and said he wanted a seat in the grandstand, he was told he was out of luck. The team physically did not have any seats left to give, not even for him.

It was better this way, though. In keeping with the way the Saints and the league operated, the owners' box bred a sort of congenial atmosphere, where people could relax and get to know one another. People who already knew one another became better friends in the owners' box. People who had never met quickly became acquainted. Kids would sit in the groundskeepers' tractors and pretend to drive. Jane Blackwell would bake brownies, Van Schley's daughter, Hannah, would wheel around Mike Veeck's daughter, Rebecca, in her stroller to visit the pig. If someone was heading for the concession stand, he or she would get something for everybody. Besides, it was the best spot in the ballpark from which to watch the baseball game.

CHAPTER EIGHT

Life Is a Game

When Marv Goldklang was in St. Paul to see his
team—about every other homestand or so—he had a favorite spot. While the Saints were taking batting practice,
starting at 4:30 before night games and lasting for about
forty-five minutes, Goldklang could be found in his button-
down shirt and dress slacks, sometimes with a tie, squinting
against the afternoon sun just in front of the third-base on-
deck circle, about halfway between the Saints' dugout and
the batting cage. His dark hair was flecked generously with
gray and was always closely cropped. He was a tall, trim
man, standing there with his arms folded and always talking
to somebody, usually one of the ballplayers. Goldklang was
happiest when he was talking to baseball players, or talking
to nearly anybody else about baseball. For him, becoming
so closely involved in the running of a team was to live vicariously through men much younger than he was, doing
what he always dreamed of doing.

That's why it hurt Goldklang so deeply when one of his
players was not doing well. When Paul Marak struggled,
Marv's pain was especially intense. Goldklang had uncov-
ered nearly every player on the Saints by himself, scouring
statistics, reading article after article, calling scouts, managers, and any other baseball person he could get to answer
the phone, trying to learn more about the people who
might play for him. And under the Northern League's
unique quota system, each team was allowed only certain
numbers of particular types of players: four veterans overall, players who had more than four years of professional

experience. Seven rookies, who had played less than about one-third of a pro season. And only one veteran pitcher. After careful searching, Paul Marak, in his eighth year of professional ball, was it for the Saints.

Once a promising pitcher in the Atlanta Braves' organization, Marak actually made it to the show, playing there for parts of two seasons before a shoulder injury threatened his career and caused the Braves to release him. It was an injury from which he would never fully recover. But Goldklang saw in Marak a genuinely nice person who wanted desperately to pitch, and who convinced Goldklang that he could still pitch, that his shoulder didn't bother him. Maybe he really thought it wouldn't. But every time Paul Marak took the mound, everybody knew it did—it was painfully obvious that every time Paul wound and threw, his right shoulder hurt intensely. By July 15, when Marv took up his position to the left of the batting cage, Marak was 1-3 in nine appearances, with an 8.36 earned run average. "I don't know what to do about Paul Marak," Goldklang said, knowing that for the Saints to contend for the league championship, the player in the veteran pitching position was going to have to do much better than Marak had done all season. "It's really difficult, because I want so much for him to succeed. But he's our veteran pitcher, and he's just not producing."

Goldklang wondered, too, about Keith Gogos. He learned about Gogos when he was emerging the winter before emerging as a .400-hitting slugger for his native Melbourne, Australia, team, a club of which Marv was part-owner. But Keith was struggling, his batting average hovering around .200 in his limited playing time at left field, designated hitter, and, infrequently, at his preferred position at first base. "He's got to decide whether he can contribute," Goldklang said, not without a little guilt. "First and foremost, he's a first baseman. In fairness to Keith, he's working hard and trying to contribute, but he's a little hamstrung by the position we're putting him in."

Maybe Pocatello, Idaho, would have been the best place for Gogos, or for Stephane Dionne, destined to live out the season as a bullpen catcher, or for some of the rookies like pitcher Eric Moran. It doesn't sound like a garden spot, and by many measures it's not—least of all by a baseball yardstick. Pocatello is an entry in the Pioneer League, a rookie-level minor-league that is a mixture of independent clubs like Pocatello and affiliated teams in Idaho, Montana, and western Canada. Many Saints had passed through the Pioneer League, some as members of the independent and now-defunct Pioneer League powerhouse Salt Lake City Trappers, and some as rookies playing there for their first professional baseball experience. In 1993 Pocatello had a sorry team—bad enough that the club's general manager had called Goldklang several times to explore the possibility of an option agreement. Similar to the arrangements between major-league parent clubs and minor-league affiliates, the Saints would option some players to Idaho, keeping their contracts and paying their salaries. If they needed to call these players up during the season they could, and they would retain rights to these players through next season so they could possibly come back and contribute in the Northern League after they'd gotten some playing experience. But it was mid-July, both the Northern League and Pioneer League seasons were nearing their midpoints, and for the most part the Saints were going to have to be content with the house they had built.

Frank Charles was struggling, and there was no reason for it. Charles had come to the Saints confident he could lead the team as its catcher, hit well, call a good game, and make his way back to a major-league organization. He knew it so well, in fact, that his subconscious decided he was already there, and he didn't have to get the job done in St. Paul. In any case, Charles' batting average hovered around—or below—.200 for the first third of the season. He wasn't throwing runners out and stopping pitches in the dirt as advertised, and he was splitting time behind the plate with Willie Smith, when Frank was supposed to be the starting catcher.

Ever since he was a freshman in high school in southern California, Frank Charles learned to expect himself and his team to do well on the baseball field. That year, his team went to the Babe Ruth World Series, and he was on a winning team every year after that until he became a pro. At first, though, baseball was merely Charles' avenue to get a college scholarship. He did get one, at Pepperdine University, a $17,000-a-year private college with a reputation for great baseball teams. But during his freshman year Frank got caught in the middle of a power struggle between two coaches at Pepperdine, and then he hurt his shoulder and broke his hand. As a sophomore, Charles realized he wasn't comfortable at Pepperdine, and his coaches released him from his scholarship and helped him get another one at California State-Fullerton, just as the team was hitting its stride on the way to the College World Series. He didn't catch much there, finding himself instead mostly at first base and designated hitter, but he hit .338 with six home runs and fifty RBI as a junior, and he thought surely he would be drafted.

He was not then, so Frank had to wait until his senior season, when the San Francisco Giants took him in the seventeenth round. If a player has college eligibility left, or if he is just finishing high school, teams will offer even their mid- and lower-level draftees five-figure signing bonuses as an enticement to skip school and play ball. As a senior with no college eligibility (thus, no bargaining power), Charles saw none of that money, accepting $2,500 in cash, $3,000 towards college tuition in the off-season, and a chance to play. He went to Everett, Washington, in the short-season Northwest League, where he caught two-thirds of the time and tore up the league at the plate in 1991, hitting .318 with nine home runs and forty-nine RBI. He was named to the Topps Rookie All-Star Team for Single A, meaning he was considered the nation's best first-year catcher in the low minors. In 1992 Charles was invited to minicamp, an honor the Giants bestowed on only forty prospects each spring, then he spent the season in San Jose of the California League, the club's top Single A farm team. There he hit

.290 and earned an honorable mention on the California League All-Star team.

But in the spring of 1993, Charles was surprised to find himself again assigned to the San Jose locker room for spring training. He had expected at least to start camp working out with the Double A players, even if he would be dropped back down to San Jose when the teams broke camp. After all, the Giants had new owners and new management, and he was looking for a fresh chance to show what he could do. Four days before camp broke, his manager called him into the player-development office, located at the back of a suite of offices behind the players' locker rooms. For a San Francisco Giants prospect, it was like a condemned prisoner taking the long, lonely walk to the gas chamber.

"You saw guys getting pulled back there all the time, and it was like, 'I'm sorry, man'," Frank remembered. "It's ironic. That same day a couple of good friends of mine who were drafted the same year as me, who I thought were good players, when I got to the park in the morning they were sitting on the curb with their bags packed, and I couldn't believe it. I told them how sorry I was, and I felt bad. As I was getting dressed, I was telling everybody that I couldn't believe they released those guys. Then the manager came and got me. The first thing I thought as I was walking back there is that they might send me back to Clinton [in the lower Single A Midwest League]. Then when I was about halfway down the hall, it hit me that this could be it. I just blanked. It was total disbelief. I was just floored, and my mouth dropped open. The only thing I could think was that I'm going to get picked up in a day or two, and I'm going to come back and shove it right up their ass. That didn't happen."

Instead, Tim Blackwell, whom Charles looked up to as a veteran major-league catcher, convinced Frank to give the Northern League a try. Once he got there, though, Charles began having trouble almost immediately, even though he became an instant heartthrob among the teeny-bopper set, with fourteen-year-old girls flocking to the ballpark just to get a look at the six-foot-four, 210 pound, darkly handsome catcher (it was attention he didn't really want, and, frankly, didn't quite understand). In part, Frank's troubles came because he expected himself to be terrific on the field, and when that didn't happen he began pushing harder and harder, until he pushed himself into a downward spiral almost too severe to pull himself out. In part, Frank was bringing onto the field his personal problems. His girlfriend, preparing to start law school back in California, had no love for baseball or any sport, and she had a hard time understanding why he needed to play the game so much if it meant they had to be apart. For his part, Frank had a difficult time at first understanding her position, and he got defensive about why he wanted to play and why he loved the game so much. There were plenty of long, upsetting phone calls across half the continent, and Charles might as well have brought the phone on the field with him, he was letting it get to him so badly. "Her family was never into sports, and her emphasis was always on school. For her to end up in a relationship with somebody whose life is a game, it's kind of a shock to see so much of that person's life revolving around a game."

But eventually, Frank's cycle had hit bottom, and two factors contributed to his upswing. First, after his girlfriend visited Minnesota and they had some long talks, each of them came to understand the other's position, and she gave Frank her blessing to give baseball all the chance he needed. Then, Blackwell benched Frank for two days straight and had a long talk with him in the middle of July. "He said, 'You're not having any fun. Why are you here? You've got to reassess why you're here. You should be here to have fun,'" Charles recalled. "He was right. I'd been moping around, and Tim said I wasn't being the leader I was when I started. I figured, this might be my last season, so why not have fun? Otherwise, I might really regret it when it was over."

Under the grandstand, in the groundskeeper's shed that opens out onto the owner's box and then to the field, sat a white casket on wheels. Inside the casket lay Mike Veeck,

Annie Huidekoper (above) shares a moment with Joe Hauser, the former Minneapolis Millers slugger, who was honored with a special day at a 1993 Saints game.

Leon Durham (left) gets to know that day's honorary bat boy before a game.

Marv Goldklang (above) says hello to Kevin Millar before a home game.

Saints manager Tim Blackwell (right) and mustache.

Actor, Saints co-owner, and first base coach-for-a-day Bill Murray (far right) butts in as Thunder Bay Whiskey Jacks manager Dan Schwam and catcher Dan Gray argue their case with umpire Ken Lehner.

Bullpen catcher Stephane Dionne discusses baseball with young fans gathered around the bullpen. Close proximity to the players was one of the best parts of the Northern League.

A familiar sight: Rick Hirtensteiner is safe at home.

Artist Andy Nelson (above) works on his mural on the outside wall of Municipal Stadium. That vendor is Tommy Green selling Dove Bars.

Sister Rosalind (right) administers lower back relief to a tense Saints fan. If the game wasn't relaxing enough, five bucks could get you a half-inning massage from the therapeutic nun.

The Lovely Gina gives a trim to a young fan during a Saints game.
A haircut was $10 and all the baseball you could watch.

Kevin Millar and Derrick Dietrich (right) make conversation with Saint the Pig. Saint's owner, Dennis Hauth, rigged up the remote-controlled three-wheeled motorcycle so the pig could motor around the basepaths to the strains of "Leader of the Pack."

Hannah Schley, (below) daughter of Northern League Director of Baseball Operations Van Schley, gets into the act of escorting Saint the Pig to deliver balls to the umpire between innings. Saint looks tiny there, but he ballooned to close to 200 pounds by the playoffs.

*Jim Eppard,
Edson Hoffman,
Kevin Millar,
Tony Darden, and
Willie Smith
(above, l–r) before
gametime on Saint
the Pig Day.*

*Pitcher Ed Stryker
(left) on
Conehead Day.*

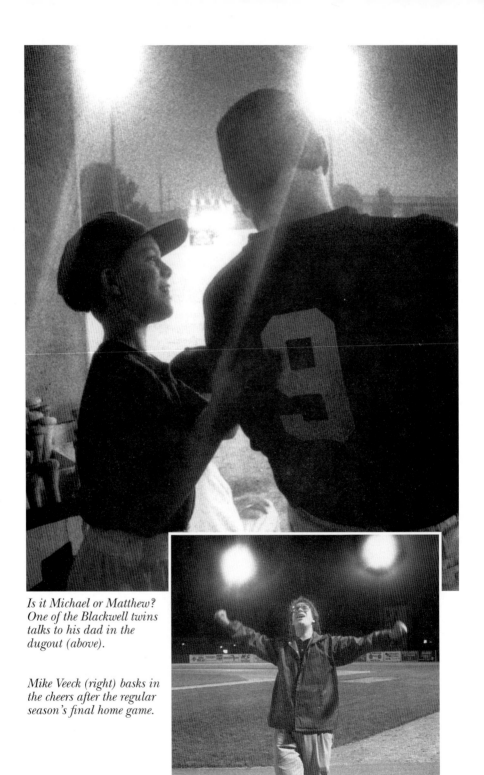

*Is it Michael or Matthew?
One of the Blackwell twins
talks to his dad in the
dugout (above).*

*Mike Veeck (right) basks in
the cheers after the regular
season's final home game.*

with a white top hat resting on his lap, wearing a red cape, and holding a black cane. However much the Minnesota Twins might have wished it, Veeck was not dead. It was just Friday, July 16. After all, the Saints did not have a home date on any Friday the Thirteenths, but Veeck got it into his head that he wanted to do a Friday the thirteenth promotion, so he was going to find the closest day he could and do it anyway. As he lay in state, Bill Fanning stood looking over the body, mulling over in his mind all the possible wisecracks.

"You didn't think I would do this, did you, Fanning?" Veeck asked.

"Are you happy to see me, or is that just a top hat on your lap?"

"Well, you do look pretty alluring when you're dead," Veeck shot back. "At least, that's what I hear."

After a Headless Horseman threw out the first pitch, Annie Huidekoper and John Spolyer wheeled Veeck out to the visitors' dugout, where he leaped out of the casket, ran toward the startled Sioux Falls Canaries, and dropped to his knees. He began waving his arms wildly and wiggling his fingers at the dugout as Creedence Clearwater Revival belted out over the public address system with, "I've Got a Spell On You."

The Saints hopped over the third baseline on the way to their positions (the superstitious nature of baseball players lends itself to a Friday the Thirteenth promotion), and they went on to beat the Canaries 8-3. Maybe it wasn't such a goofy idea after all.

Marv Goldklang took his position near the batting cage the next day, but his arms were not folded comfortably in front of him. They were stuffed deep in his pockets. Goldklang was angry. "The scouts are calling and asking for information, this is the hottest ticket in town, the Twins are getting anxious about us—the word is out that the quality of baseball is about at Double A, that we are something to be taken seriously."

Funny, but Goldklang doesn't look anything like Rodney Dangerfield. But he was stricken with a severe case of "We Don't Get No Respect." The Minneapolis *Star Tribune*, the *St. Paul Pioneer Press*, the local TV and radio stations, *Baseball America*, *The Sporting News*, *USA Today Baseball Weekly*—you name the media outlet, and Marv Goldklang felt the Northern League and its star attraction, the St. Paul Saints, were being shortchanged there. "See, Miles is such a nice guy, he won't say anything," Marv fumed. "But the story you aren't reading—and the story they're missing—is how this league is fundamentally changing the way major-league teams develop players."

He was ranting, but he was right. The media—local and national—was giving the Northern League the shaft. The *Star Tribune* took daily game stories from Dave Wright who, though a nice guy and a very capable media relations director, was still a public relations flak (that's not necessarily bad, it's just his job), and packaged them as "Special to the Star Tribune," so the paper's report was inherently biased and compromised, written as it was by a St. Paul Saints employee. The paper—the largest within three hundred miles in any direction—ostensibly had a beat writer, Eric Pate, who all but refused to write game stories and then did features only when he felt like it and had nothing else to do (including, to the paper's credit, a massive three-page Sunday text and photo spread), and even then he seemed more concerned with slipping in the parts of a story that would make people salivate rather than the parts that actually related to the actual story. Sometimes what he wrote was accurate. The *Pioneer Press* tried, and often failed, to assign a beat writer to all the home games, and had a stringer covering the team on the road. But every night the paper asked for three hundred words—about six paragraphs—and it was a special day when it ran half of that in the paper.

The local columnists, most of whom relied on the Minnesota Twins for free press-box food and good quotes for six months out of the year, asked Twins general manager Andy MacPhail what he thought of the Saints and took his opinion to heart. Sid Hartman, the dean of the Twin

Cities sports columnists (that means he's been there forever, beholden to dozens of friends in the local establishment, regardless of whether he can actually write), never bothered to show up at a Northern League game, but he felt compelled to ignore the club in his *Star Tribune* column and postulate on his weekly radio show that the league would be dead by July 3 (the Saints sold out that night). Patrick Reusse, the *Star Tribune's* other big-wheel columnist, at least gave the Saints a chance, attending a couple of games and writing columns about them, but he focused on what the team and the league didn't have, rather than on what they did have. For example, he fixated on the fact that the Saints had little home-run power, but he missed the fact that the team hit .286 and scored more than five and a half runs a game while allowing their opponents fewer than four and a half runs a game. *St. Paul Pioneer Press* star sports columnist Bob Sansevere called the Northern League talent "dental-floss thin" before he ever saw a game (he never asked anybody, but what he actually had observed was a league tryout, from which only one hopeful out of more than 150 was signed). "'Severe' is right," Veeck would say later, referring to the columnist's name. Yet in the end, even Sansevere kept coming back, because he was having a good time.

Goldklang's beef with *Baseball America* was not quite as valid—the baseball trade publication did have a stringer assigned to cover the league in every issue, and it sent an editor, Mike Berardino, to travel the league for a week and write an extensive feature about the Northern League phenomenon: two full tabloid pages and a cover photo of Leon Durham. The regular Northern League column was buried with reports of the Japanese and Mexican leagues, for lack of a better spot, and it was scrunched together with the report of the Frontier League, the other independent league that summer. But the Frontier League might as well have been called the Bush League. The entire league missed its first payroll, even though players made a measly $300 a month plus room and board. Two of the eight teams folded after the first month, and one manager was fired for keeping balls rejected by the umpire so he could replace the club's worn-out batting practice balls. One team played its home games at a high school park with a gravel infield, and another club had no home field at all, playing all sixty of its games on the road.

"I mean, the Frontier League, come on," Goldklang fumed. "They put us on the same page as the foreign leagues. We're better than that. We should be on our own page."

On July 18, with the Saints clinging to a slim hope of still winning the second-half crown, Blackwell and Goldklang agreed they would give Paul Marak one last chance to show he could still pitch. It was a few more chances than Marak reasonably could have expected, but everybody liked the reserved, bearded righthander, and they wanted to do everything they could for him. Marak came in with one out in the ninth, in a game the Saints were already losing to Sioux City 7-3. With a runner on first, Marak gave up a double, then a single, letting in two more runs before retiring the final two batters. After the game, his earned run average had climbed again, to 9.77.

When the team boarded the bus the next morning for the drive to Sioux Falls, Marak was gone.

In Marak's place was Don Heinkel, a lanky, dark-haired pitcher with a thin face and a quick smile. It was far from Heinkel's first minor-league bus trip—that had come more than a decade earlier, as Ronald Reagan was just getting used to his Oval Office chair in 1982, and Don began his pro career. As four small television screens hanging underneath the overhead luggage racks began to flicker with the image of the movie "Bull Durham" that was playing in the VCR, Heinkel couldn't hide a chuckle. It was all so true: the eternal bus rides, the card games, the vain attempts to sleep in a cramped coach seat, the hopes of the players mixed with the bitter realities of life on the road. For Don Heinkel, though, it was a way of life with a finite time limit. It had to be that way for a guy who was trying to support a wife and four kids, with a fifth on the way, on some savings and a $1,400 monthly Northern League salary. After 12 years of trying—and a lot of frustrations mixed with some success—Don and his wife, Angela, had decided this would be his last pro season. Unless, Heinkel noted, that million-to-one shot came through and a club offered him another shot at the big leagues.

He had had a taste of that once. After being drafted by the Tigers in the thirtieth round of the 1982 draft (or, as Heinkel liked to say, "In the first round—after the twenty-ninth"), he shot through Single A in record speed, winding up in Birmingham, Alabama, and Double A before his first year was over. It was there that he rediscovered his faith, became a devout Christian, and met Angela, a minister's daughter. Heinkel, his growing family in tow, bounced between Double A and Triple A until 1988, when he broke camp with the Tigers and spent most of the season in Detroit, making twenty-one relief appearances and finishing with a 3.96 ERA and one save. As he was preparing for another season of winter ball (Heinkel and his family moved south to Puerto Rico or Mexico nearly every winter so he could play there and keep his skills sharp), he called his team and asked what skills they wanted him to focus on. The Tigers informed Heinkel he could work on whatever he wanted, because they were releasing him.

Unfazed, Don went to Puerto Rico anyway, played well, and signed with the Cardinals for 1989, his second season in the show. His shoulder started to hurt that May, and by July he was on an operating table, with a scalpel-wielding surgeon preparing to end Heinkel's season and, hopefully, to extend his career.

Those two years in the big leagues, with the luxurious salaries and first-class travel, had whetted Don's appetite for more, so he did everything he could to keep playing, even after the Cardinals had released him after the 1990 season, the Indians had released him after he spent 1991 with their Double A club, and he couldn't find any other opportunities in the United States. It was off to Italy for the Heinkel brood, where Don played for six months. After that, he got a chance to play in the Mexican Summer League, where he played well and even tossed a perfect game. He still wanted that one last chance to make it back to the majors, but the Heinkels' savings from his two major-league seasons were running low, and the time was coming to make a decision. San Diego gave Heinkel a shot, sending him to their Double A team in Wichita. He was a natural starter, and he struggled in his relief role. Heinkel's fastball never pushed past the mid-eighties even on his best days, so he relied on faking hitters out with finesse, using a forkball and a sidearm knuckle curve. When those pitches worked, even the best batters didn't know how to hit Heinkel. But on bad days just about anybody could tee off on him. He often needed the cushion of a few innings to even out a rocky performance and give his offense a chance to produce some run support, something he didn't get as a reliever. When the Padres released Heinkel at the end of June, he headed back to Birmingham and prepared to go on with his life with his wife and soon-to-be five children, getting ready, at age thirty-three, to head to medical school, hoping to become a doctor by his fortieth birthday.

But, like the rest of his new teammates, Don received a call from Marv Goldklang, and simply couldn't resist the urge to play baseball again. And sit through those interminable bus rides.

CHAPTER NINE

Can't Go Out on a Positive Note

By July 24, there were only two games left in the first half, and the Saints, with a 19-15 record, were two games behind the Rochester Aces for the split season's first title and the final berth in the playoffs. The year's first thirty-four games had been a combination of exhilaration—mostly early, when the Saints rushed to a 6-0 start and a big lead over the rest of the league—and frustration, as the club struggled to play .500 ball for the rest of the way and to stay atop the Northern League standings. The pressure—most of it self-imposed as the players strove for a championship ring, and to catch the attention of a scout who could lift them out of the Northern League and back into organized baseball—was beginning to weigh on the team, and the ends of this taut rope were beginning to fray.

In this atmosphere, or probably because of it, Tim Blackwell was talking again in the dugout before the game. Not to anybody in particular, but to whomever happened to be sitting there and listening. It was the manager's way of lecturing without lecturing, of preaching his gospel of love for the game without necessarily forcing anybody to listen. "You know, when you're carrying your lunch box, one of those big Igloos with the six-pack in it," he said, using the bucket of batting-practice balls as his imaginary Igloo, "you don't run with that lunch box to punch the clock. You've got to realize, every person who is out there who bought a ticket, wants to be doing what you're doing. You're playing baseball."

"Are you saying we should hustle out there?" Jim Eppard asked, playing Costello to Blackwell's Abbott.

"Even the worst player can hustle. It's not that hard. We're doing something for a living that's fun. We can run to work because we're doing something anybody else would do for free."

That was a thoughtful lesson from Blackwell, but it didn't do much to alleviate the strain the Saints' players felt. They all knew they had the best team in the league, and they were playing to sold-out houses every night, yet they couldn't seem to string two victories together. And since they were human beings, these players began blaming one another. Pitchers blamed hitters for a lack of run support. Hitters blamed pitchers for not being able to get the big out.

On July 26, the day after the first half of the season ended with the Saints two games behind the Aces, before batting practice, the Saints position players gathered in a circle in shallow left field, and, with Jim Eppard in the middle acting as a sort of facilitator, they had it out. The goal was to stop blaming each other and to try to work together. The second half of the season would begin with every team's record at 0-0, and they had thirty-six games to get things right and win the opportunity to challenge Rochester in the playoffs. "We've got to work together as a team," Eppard said over and over, straddling his dual role as the team's hitting coach and a first baseman and designated hitter. This was Eppard's twelfth year as a pro, his first as he made his transition to a coach, and he was trying to use his experience as a career .300 hitter who had won five minor-league batting titles and who had spent parts of four major-league seasons with the California Angels and the Toronto Blue Jays, to help mediate the clashes among twenty-two very different personalities.

Rick Hirtensteiner, who was one of the Saints who knew what it's like to play ball in Triple A, however briefly, and who had one of the best chances to make it to the big-leagues, urged his fellow hitters to take the responsibility upon themselves, and to stop shuffling it around to others.

"We can't rely on the pitchers to do it all. Obviously, we've got the best team in the league. We should've won the first half by ten games."

The meeting seemed to work. The Saints clobbered the Duluth Dukes 8-4, collecting thirteen hits and getting twenty-six baserunners, while four Saints pitchers scattered twelve hits and walked only two. The next night, though, they lost 9-8. The night after that, they won 15-1. Then came the Sioux Falls series, and the Saints realized that solving their problems would take more than a bonding circle in the Municipal Stadium outfield.

Simply put, the Canaries pasted the Saints two out of three, and St. Paul barely survived in that one game they won. It wasn't like St. Paul didn't hit the ball, though. In the three-game set they scored eight, nine, and ten runs respectively. In the second game Leon Durham celebrated his birthday by drilling two impressive home runs: a rope over the batter's eye in dead center, and a towering rocket to right that leaped the barbed-wire fence around the firefighter training facility, bounced twice on the grass, and rolled on the concrete almost to the training building, more than five hundred feet away. But they gave up thirteen, eight, and twelve runs, respectively. The pitching was falling apart.

Michael Mimbs was one of the pitchers whose performances was beginning to fray. Mimbs, once one of the hottest pitching prospects in the minor leagues as part of the Dodgers system, started the season 5-0 with a 2.16 ERA. (He also became part of baseball trivia when he was drafted in consecutive rounds with his identical twin brother, Mark, also by the Dodgers. But Mark, after an atrocious season in Double A, was still with the Dodgers; Mike, after pitching well, was in St. Paul.) During the first part of the season, Mike was nothing short of unhittable, and his control was superb. But baseball players with talent who love the game might be able to continue a run like that merely on adrenaline and emotion. Players who view baseball as a job are prone to the kinds of concentration lapses that Mimbs suffered.

Mike, a fair-haired, classic-featured American proto-type with a drawl typical of his Macon, Georgia, home, was upset when the season began and he found out that at $1,100 a month, he would not be the highest paid pitcher on the team (he missed by $300 a month). When he found out how wealthy Marv Goldklang was, Mimbs was even more miffed that he was not paid better. Arguments that the league had a $66,000 team salary cap for the year—an average of $1,000 per month per player—did nothing to sway him. He was angry when anybody fielding behind him made an error. Even when no one made an error and a ball still found its way through the infield, Mimbs found reasons to deflect the blame. "Mike Mimbs has never given up a hit that was his fault," was the way one frustrated St. Paul front-office figure put it, after Mimbs had exasperated the team once too often. Mimbs complained that the team didn't find him an apartment and he had to do it on his own (whether Goldklang promised this perk will forever be in dispute). He groused when the team was stuck with what he thought (correctly) to be a substandard bus, and effectively worked on his own to secure a better one, complete with a VCR. The front office only found out about it when they got the bill for the deluxe coach. While they might have wanted their players to travel in comfort, the extra tab courtesy of Mike Mimbs was a bit of a shock. His actions during the summer of 1993 made the St. Paul Saints understand why the Dodgers—an organization with a reputation for pampering even its most arrogant talent—released a player with such an impressive arm. Even at 5-0, Mike Mimbs could be more trouble than he was worth.

So when Mimbs got drilled by Sioux Falls and sulked back to the dugout, he was looking for someone to blame. The bad news for him was that the tension level in the Saints clubhouse was as taut as a piano wire, and nobody was in the mood for Mimbs' complaints, least of all trainer Dave Fricke, and especially about Tommy Raffo.

○ ○ ○

Tom Raffo was a clubhouse favorite, even though most people considered themselves fortunate to get more than three sentences at a time out of the reserved southerner. A Florida native, Raffo had played his college baseball at Mississippi State University, and he did well enough that he thought he would be drafted by a major-league organization in 1990.

It came as a surprise to Raffo, then, that he was drafted by some guy named Marv Goldklang for his Miami Miracle, then an independent team in the Florida State League. The Miracle was the only independent club that was at the time allowed to draft with the big guys, and they picked Tommy in the eighth round. That put Raffo in a unique situation. the Florida State League is traditionally the strongest Single A league in the game, and while most rookies go to a rookie or low-A league, Raffo started his career facing top pitching every day. He struggled early, but picked up his performance at the end of that first season, hit .258 for the year, and wound up having his contract purchased by the Cincinnati Reds.

Larry Bideau, the Reds' player-development director who had signed Raffo, was fired a week later. As happens so often in baseball, the person who was looking out for Tommy's interests within the organization was out knocking on doors looking for a job, while he had to impress a new regime with his talents. He did that as well as he could, playing impressively in the instructional league and hitting .277 with thirteen home runs as the starting first baseman at Charleston, West Virginia, in the Single A South Atlantic League. He spent the spring working out in the Reds' Double A camp, but he was bumped back to Single A by a highly-touted rookie, and he had to play in Cincinnati's Midwest League city, Cedar Rapids, Iowa. The Reds wanted Raffo to split his time between designated hitter and first base—a frustrating prospect for someone who wanted to move up as a first baseman. Despite that, and despite a thumb injury that forced Raffo to sit out almost half the season, he played well, hitting .302. During the off-season, Tommy arranged his schedule at a Mississippi savings and loan so he could work out every morning and every afternoon. He was determined to spend the next season, at the age of twenty-five, in Double A, bent on proving to the Reds what he had already proven to himself: that he could play baseball, and that he deserved the chance to show that at a higher level.

Raffo got to spring training and, by his account, played impressively. But the Reds, with an entirely new regime in place again, didn't see that. "They called me in," he remembered, "and they said I had a great spring, I was doing well, I just wasn't the person for the job. After we kept talking for a while, they did ask if I wanted to go back to Cedar Rapids. I said, 'Well, I've proven everything I can prove at that level.' They said, 'We didn't think you wanted to go back, so we're going to let you go. Or do you want to go back?' Those were the words." Raffo didn't want to go back, but still he wanted to play. He and his wife, Paula, had no children, and they were enjoying living in new places every year, meeting new people, having few responsibilities during the seasons except doing their jobs and living for themselves. When they settled down to permanent careers and had children, those options would be gone, and they were determined to take advantage of them while they could. Besides, Raffo was not ready to give up baseball.

"You have to remember, this is a dream, and it's something when you're a kid, you're sitting there saying, 'This is what I want to do.' And you realize you've got the ability to work for it and to keep going for it. You've got to say, 'I can't go out on a positive note.' Now, if I would have had a bad spring training, or if I didn't do well the year before, OK. Let me go into the banking industry, let me do my job. But no."

Fortunately for Tom Raffo, he had been originally drafted by Marv Goldklang. Goldklang was fiercely loyal to his draft picks, and when he saw that Raffo was available, he didn't hesitate to get in contact with him and offer him a spot on the St. Paul Saints. Raffo took the job, even though he would be one of four potential first basemen, and even though he would play only a handful of innings at that position. Using his power to always see the positive side of a situation, Raffo told himself that he would learn a new position, left field, and he would get a chance to play every day.

His hip flexor muscle did not cooperate, though. One July day Raffo was legging out a ground ball to first when he suddenly slowed before he reached the base. He limped back to the dugout, trainer Fricke beside him, and did not step onto the field to compete for the next two weeks, a long time in a season only twelve weeks long. Even after that, the painful injury—which never affected his potent, consistent swing—prevented Raffo from running at full speed for most of the season. But the reason Tommy Raffo was a professional baseball player in the first place was his hitting ability; he had a gift for seeing a baseball and for staying cool under pressure that allowed him to get hits in clutch situations that usually floored other players. For that reason, Tim Blackwell was willing to stay with Raffo, even if he was only running at seventy-five percent speed, and only then with considerable pain.

Mike Mimbs had stared in disbelief from the mound earlier in the game as Raffo barely jogged to a fly ball that seemed perfectly catchable. Raffo had cost Mimbs a baserunner. So when Fricke iced the pitcher's arm after his early exit (four innings, five runs, nine hits), Mimbs asked him why Raffo was still playing, even though he was obviously in pain. Fricke, who was in charge of Raffo's rehabilitation, was the wrong person to push on this issue.

"He almost walked to that fly ball in left," Mimbs said, correctly and legitimately.

But Fricke exploded. "You don't know what you're talking about! You don't know anything about it!" He jabbed his finger in the air again and again towards Mimbs, who backed away in surprise at the ferocity of the trainer's reaction. "You just get your facts straight. Just get your facts straight."

Later Blackwell told Mimbs, with as clear a message as the manager could provide without beating the pitcher over the head, that he hoped Mimbs was not grooving pitches down the middle and giving up hits on purpose.

○ ○ ○

When a team's pitching drops in the toilet, what else is a manager to do but send one of his reserve left fielders to the mound?

It should be noted, first, that Keith Gogos is not just some ordinary left fielder who sauntered to a pitcher's mound and tried to throw strikes. He had been a bona fide pitching prospect for the Montreal Expos, who made it all the way to Double A before his left elbow finally rebelled and said, "No more." The injury forced Gogos to stop snapping his arm to make the ball break in the way that had been paving his path to the major leagues. Throwing more than a few curveballs in a row became an act of intense pain. It was only then, in his native Australia that Keith picked up a bat and discovered he could hit tremendous home runs.

Gogos would have done well to remember that in late July, when the Saints' pitching staff was giving up more than ten hits a game—this was not a good time to joke to Tim Blackwell about pitching. But Keith didn't think about that as Blackie passed him in the dugout, with the Saints down to the Sioux Falls Canaries 13-6 in the fifth inning. Keith began flexing his arm and, with a smile so wide you could see his wad of chew, said, "Well, Blackie, I think I'm ready to go a couple of innings."

"Well, get to the bullpen and start warming up." Gogos looked at Blackwell, dumbfounded, as if the manager had just confused him for somebody else. "I'm serious," Blackwell explained. So Gogos did. He entered a game that the Saints had written off as a disaster, and he pitched two excellent innings. Three hits, three walks, one strikeout (Pedro Guerrero, looking at the first three pitches: a slider, change-up, and curve, right in a row), and no runs. Forty-seven pitches—forty-seven more pitches than Gogos had thrown in a game in three years, but it was enough for him to re-member what was, and what might have been.

○ ○ ○

The fact that Keith Gogos discovered baseball was incredible enough. The fact that he was discovered by baseball is more incredible still. Enough has been written over the years about American kids who see their first baseball game and are inextricably hooked. You don't read much about that happening half a world away, where baseball is still in its infancy. But in 1983, as a twelve-year-old living in his native Melbourne, Australia, a friend came over to Gogos's house with a videotape of the 1983 All-Star Game, with Toronto Blue Jays pitcher Dave Stieb on the mound. That was all Gogos needed to see. From that day forward Keith went down the street to a nearby park, three or four times a day, and threw a baseball as hard as he could, over and over again, snapping his wrist and contorting his elbow until he taught himself to throw a curveball. Since so few people in Australia knew, or cared, anything about baseball, nobody told him that was a good way to ruin his arm. So young Gogos, who spent most of his first eight years on his parents' native, sublime Greek island of Santorini (where there was even *less* interest in baseball than Down Under), pitched and pitched and pitched.

As Keith entered high school in Melbourne, baseball started to catch on in his country, and he got the opportunity to play on an all-star team that traveled to California to play games and attend clinics. If he ever doubted that he wanted to be a professional baseball player, it was because he had never attended a major-league game in person. After sitting through nine innings at the Oakland-Alameda County Coliseum, "That nailed down what I was going to do with my life. After I saw that game, I said, 'That's what I'm going to do with my life.' Not once did I ever think about doing something else."

That might have been too bad for Gogos, because he was developing into quite an Australian Rules Football player. So good, in fact, that the Melbourne Demons of the Australian National Football League signed him to a six-figure contract to play that sport that appears late-night on ESPN, with the players seeming to run raggedly up and down the field, beating the hell out of one another, until one of the white-coated officials steps forward and points both fingers from his waist like an Old West gunslinger.

It was one of the zeniths of sports in his country (and worth plenty of money, too), but Gogos told the Demons to take a hike. He forsook his signed contract because the Montreal Expos had come calling. An Expos scout had seen Gogos pitch, had clocked his fastball at ninety-two miles an hour, and had seen how he snapped the curve. In 1988 Montreal signed him and sent him to West Palm Beach in the rookie Gulf Coast League, where Keith ran headlong into American food.

Australians must habitually eat healthier than Americans, because once Gogos set foot in the United States he gained fifteen pounds on the junk he was eating. In the first month of his first season he had no earned run average: he went thirty innings without letting a runner score. But as his waist-line expanded, so did his ERA, to 7.31 by the end of the second month. Keith did manage to get his eating habits in check by the season's third and final month, and he finished the season with a 3.35 ERA. Because of his yo-yo first year, and because of immigration snafus that made him late to report for spring training, Gogos started his second season in the rookie league as well. But he was quickly moved up— to Jacksonville, the Expo's Double A affiliate. He was pitching well there, getting hitters out, when one day as he was trying to throw one of those curveballs he had perfected against a Melbourne brick wall, he felt a twinge. But Gogos was finally on the road to where he wanted to be, and he was so afraid of seeing his path diverted that he committed the pitcher's cardinal sin: he didn't tell anybody his arm hurt. He tried to pitch through it. Of course, that only made the problem worse. Finally, as Keith threw a pitch, his elbow simply popped out of its socket. He couldn't hide that, with his left arm dangling helplessly by his side.

The Expos said he needed surgery, and there would be a fifty-fifty chance he would pitch again. Those odds were not good enough for Gogos, and he refused the surgery. He went to spring training with the California Angels in 1990 as a pitcher, but his elbow gave way again. Keith had to get on a plane and spend the twenty-four-hour flight back to Australia thinking about whether he would ever play baseball again. Gogos decided he had to play again; all that was left was to find a way to do it. So he picked up a bat and tried hitting the ball. He could, he discovered, hit the ball a very long way. Long enough that Boston, Oakland, and the New York Yankees were interested in signing him for the 1991 season as a first baseman and a hitter (mostly as a hitter).

In the meantime Keith had met and fallen in love with the future Michelle Gogos, who was a Los Angeles native and a U.S. citizen. They were married, and his immigration problems started in earnest. The Immigration and Naturalization Service thought that maybe Gogos had entered the country illegally before he was married; they suspected, therefore, that he and Michelle might have enlisted into a green-card marriage, a union of convenience so that Keith could stay in the United States. At first Gogos was offended by the accusation. As time went on, however, he was too worn down by the agonizing immigration process to feel any emotion. Worse still, the two years of dallying by the INS cost Gogos, when he was twenty-one and twenty-two, two valuable years of prime playing time. In essence, the bureaucracy ruined his next best chance at a baseball career. Meanwhile, Gogos played semipro baseball and then went back to Australia and played for Melbourne in the fledgling Australian professional baseball league (a team owned in part by the omnipresent Marv Goldklang). Since he hit .421 with twenty-one home runs in forty-eight games while leading the Monarchs to the national title, he caught the attention of the Florida Marlins, who said they were interested but couldn't sign him right then. The team that could sign him right then was the St. Paul Saints.

But in St. Paul, Gogos was the third-string left fielder and the fourth-string first baseman. If hitters become proficient with practice, it was no wonder that Gogos was hitting in the low .200s; sitting on the bench allows a player time to ponder his future, but it doesn't do much for one's ability to see the spin on a slider. Keith Gogos was neither willing nor able to accept the end of baseball in his life, but he was becoming resigned to the fact that his future would not be helped by his year in the Northern League.

During all this business of the Saints trying to win a Northern League playoff spot, Mike Mimbs had other, more important things to worry about. The Kansas City Royals had called his agent and said they were considering signing Mimbs to fill an empty spot in their Double A roster at Memphis. Mimbs was so anxious to get out of St. Paul and back into organized baseball he practically hopped down the runway to the pay phone to call back his agent.

It was true, said the agent, who, Mimbs was quick to point out, lived in Hollywood and had extensive connections in the film industry, whatever that could do to help a ballplayer (though it was an impressive credential to Mimbs).The Royals just needed a few days to think about their options, to consider whether they'd rather bring up a young pitcher from Single A to give him some experience at a higher level. But as far as Mimbs was concerned, it was a done deal, and soon he would be a Kansas City Royal.

One of Mike Mimbs' problems in his evolution as a baseball player was that he never knew when to keep quiet. He never knew to display the tact that came with working in any organization where those above you could either make you a star or make you miserable. In a small world like baseball, where there aren't that many people, and they all know each other, a loose tongue can ruin a player's reputation. And a bad reputation can quickly obscure a tremendous talent. In the summer of 1993, Mike Mimbs was right on the cusp of that happening to him. He was a genuinely nice person, with a fiancé who loved him, and a soft spot for kids who walked up to him and asked for pitching advice, and a need and desire to be liked. But through what he said, and how he acted, that often did not come through to people. Already that year he had gone straight over the heads of Bill Fanning, the general manager, and Mike Veeck, the president, to complain to Marv Goldklang, the chairman, about his apartment situation. That episode had soured Veeck on the righthander and had earned Mimbs a screaming lecture from Fanning, who was slow to anger but difficult to stop once he got started. Mimbs also made no secret to anybody about his dissatisfaction with his salary, and how he knew a rich guy like Goldklang could afford more. And he boasted to a newspaper reporter that he would be out of the Northern League and on to bigger things by July.

It looked as if his prediction might come true, albeit a month later. But there was still the issue of whether the Royals indeed wanted to sign Mimbs, and then of the Saints negotiating a sale price for his contract. Mimbs, who didn't trust Goldklang to look out for his best interests, wondered openly whether Marv would be fair about dealing with Kansas City, or whether he would hold out for a lot of money just to spite him, or to help the Saints' playoff chances by keeping the lefthander around through the end of the season. He refused to believe the people who told him that Goldklang was a fair main, and that he was genuinely concerned with placing every one of his players with a major-league organization, no matter what the cost to his team's chances. Mimbs didn't accept the argument that whether the Saints negotiated $3,000 or $5,000 or even $10,000 for a contract sale, this was not a big revenue producer, especially when compared to the prestige the Northern League gained every time it sold a player to the big leagues. And it never seemed to occur to Mimbs that he had so alienated the front office, his manager, and his teammates that the Saints would take just about any amount to sell his contract.

The possibility of signing with the Royals had gotten into his head. After starting out as the league's most dominating pitcher with five straight victories, Mimbs began pitching like someone preoccupied. "It's in my head," he admitted after a string of bad outings that included a loss, a couple of ugly no-decisions, and a victory in a slugfest, while his earned run average climbed past 3.6. But all of Mimbs' talking and speculating and wondering was moot. The Royals never called back, and eventually they called up one of their Single A players. Mimbs would have to erase this episode from his head and begin concentrating again on the team he was already playing for.

CHAPTER TEN

Miraculous Cacophony

Few people were surprised when the St. Paul Saints sold out their June 18 home opener when tickets went on sale the month before. It did not come as a shock to many, in fact, when the entire three-game opening weekend was a sellout. The Saints and the Northern League were a novelty, and novelties generally attract a rush of attention right at the start; everybody wants to come out and see what the fuss is all about, especially when part of the novelty is the return of outdoor baseball, something thousands of Minnesota baseball fans had been pining for for more than a decade. But the real sign of a success is what happens in the second week, and the second month, and the second half of a season. And that's when the Saints showed they were a bona fide phenomenon. They drew well during the second week. They drew better the second month. For the second half, they drew as well as was physically possible without putting more seats in Municipal Stadium. Capacity for Municipal Stadium was officially listed at 5,069. Some other minor-league ballparks, in order to make their attendance figures look more impressive, either give away large numbers of tickets (as the Salt Lake Trappers did on their way to setting short-season attendance records), or they simply fudge their numbers. The Saints, on the other hand, set their announced sellout number, but sold as many as 5,200 tickets for some games, cramming as many fans as they could into the general admission sections. They actually undercounted their crowds on some nights.

That was not supposed to happen when the season began. Chairman Marv Goldklang, president Mike Veeck, and general manager Bill Fanning sat down and figured they would need to coax 2,200 fans a night through the turnstiles to break even. They had convinced the city to add two thousand bleacher seats to the park at the beginning of the season because they thought that on some nights they would do better than that, and they would even sell out a five-thousand-seat house on special nights like the Fourth of July, or on nights when some certain zany promotion was on. But, on the whole, they decided that 2,200 per night was not an unreasonable expectation for this first season. After all, the Fort Myers Miracle of the Florida State League, which Goldklang owned and Veeck ran, was lucky to draw a thousand a night, and that team had benefit of the same Veeckian stunts as did St. Paul. So after the initial euphoria of that first weekend, when the Saints took three straight from the hapless Thunder Bay Whiskey Jacks in front of full houses every game, the club expected attendance to die down a bit. Maybe settle down closer to their projected levels. The Saints management was astounded, then, when people kept coming. Even in the beginning of the season, when the temperature was often chilly and every game seemed to bring on either drizzle or the threat of rain, the stands were still full of people bent on seeing the Saints play baseball. It was in those first few weeks, in fact, that the team logged its only game of the year where the attendance dropped below four thousand, on a cold, windy, misty night, when even the players didn't want to be there.

The Minneapolis-St. Paul metropolitan area is a large one, with more than 2.5 million people living in the two cities and their outlying suburbs. But despite the big-city numbers, Twin Citians have clung to their self-image as a small, close-knit community. In many ways, those days were long past—Minneapolis had big-city crime, big-city poverty, big-city commerce, and big-city amenities such as arts and major-league sports—but word of mouth was still at least as important in St. Paul and Minneapolis as it was in any

25,000-person burg. And when the talk began spreading about what it was like to be at a St. Paul Saints game, about how much fun it was, about the between-inning antics, and the feel once again of outdoor baseball, interest in the team and the Northern League did not shrink, it grew. Logic about these matters was rendered moot as people began queuing up at the ticket window and clogging the Saints office with phone calls to order tickets. The Saints, all of a sudden, had become hip. Before anybody could figure out what happened, they were *the* ticket in the Twin Cities.

The Broadway smashes "Phantom of the Opera" and "Miss Saigon" were on their way to town. So what? The Twins were still playing out their string at the Metrodome. Who cares? The NFL Vikings and NBA Timberwolves were hawking tickets for the starts of their seasons. We'll think about them later.

The Saints became so chic that there were actually scalpers selling game tickets with face values of three, five, and six dollars for upwards of ten or twelve bucks. People were thumbing through their Rolodexes for someone they knew who might have a connection with the team so they could get tickets. The crush was so overwhelming that ticket manager Stephanie Baumgartner finally stopped phone sales in the Saints office and farmed the business out to Ticketmaster, the computerized ticket-selling service that adds a charge to each admission. Public address announcer Al Frechtman told the assembled throng one night that Ticketmaster was "legalized scalping," and the Saints believed that, but they had no choice. Too many people wanted tickets, and too few people worked in the Saints office to handle the crush.

The demand was so great, in fact, that by the time the second half of the season started on July 27, only a handful of general-admission tickets remained for three of thirty-five second-half games, plus one night in August that featured a postgame concert and higher ticket prices and was selling poorly. Two days into the second half, all the seats for those three games were gone. The Saints had filled the park to capacity for each of the eight games before the halfway mark, and the second half of the season was sold out in advance.

The eleven people who crammed themselves into the four offices and the entryway of the area below the Municipal Stadium bleachers did so not because they thought they were latching onto the next big thing. They were looking for a job they could love, and they loved the idea of the St. Paul Saints and the Northern League.

Mike Veeck, the team president, one-third owner, and heir to the throne of baseball irreverence, wanted a place to ply his trade without interference from the commissioner of baseball, or from anybody else in organized baseball who could possibly keep him from bringing fans into the stands and giving them a good time.

General manager Bill Fanning was first a stockbroker and then a banker in Denver. But he chucked both of those lucrative careers because he was not happy; he was a baseball person at heart, and he took a low-level job with the Triple A Denver Zephyrs to satiate his need. He moved on to jobs at clubs in Spokane and Wichita before finally landing the big job in St. Paul, where he ran the business operations of the club.

Dave Wright was the media relations director, and in him the Saints found someone who had a knowledge of Minnesota sports and the Twin Cities media that was nearly unmatched. Of course, it came in a package that was sometimes manic and prone to melodrama, but Wright was tireless in his pursuit for more press for his team. The key to keeping the media happy is massaging egos, and Wright understood that; he massaged with impunity, and the Saints benefitted from it.

Annie Huidekoper signed on as a part-time employee months before the season began, anxious to be near what she considered an important event. She was a Boston Red Sox fan of long standing, and as far as she was concerned, playing baseball indoors, in climate-controlled comfort, was akin to sacrilege in the Temple of Baseball. The game was far too important to Annie to let it dissolve to that point, so she wanted to be a part of the St. Paul Saints' effort to help restore the sport to its rightful status in the Twin Cities, outdoors and spontaneous. But once the season drew near, there was no such thing as a part-time employee at Municipal Stadium; by the time the first home game came around, even a forty-hour week was all but a memory. For her love of baseball and the Saints, Huidekoper took to her task as the club's community relations director, running the fan-services booth in the concourse and making sure promotions went off as they were supposed to. It was Annie's job, for example, to make sure the National-Anthem singers found their way to the field and had Saints hats on their heads when they performed—even the string quartet dressed in formal wear. It was more work than she had ever imagined, and during games she sometimes looked like someone who was working three jobs instead of one. At Gabe's after the games, though, she had time to be happy that she got to be near baseball every day.

Stephanie Baumgartner was hired to answer phones and handle clerical duties way back when the field was covered with snow and the Saints had only two phone lines. By the time there were eight lines ringing constantly, she had become the ticket manager. It was a job she didn't necessarily want, but one she took anyway, almost by default. Coming in cold turkey, she had to coordinate the logistics of selling and distributing tickets for one of the most successful teams in baseball. Stephanie was trying to nurture a stained relationship, and she and Fanning occasionally clashed. But she was there every afternoon, and she had to tell sometimes belligerent would-be spectators that the game was sold out, and maybe they should try to come the next day two hours before game time, when about five hundred returned or unclaimed presale tickets went on sale every home date.

It might have seemed before the season began that a sales staff of three might be more than enough for a fledgling minor-league club like the Saints. But Tom Whaley, Pete Orme, and Dan Craighead never lacked for things to do. Because when they weren't entertaining offers for promotions or advertising from area businesses—indeed, the accounts sometimes seemed to come to them, not the other way around—they were helping sell T-shirts or filling ticket orders or helping stock the concession stands when there weren't enough other people to do it. It was a change for all three of them—Whaley was a practicing attorney who still kept his law office open even as he spent his days and nights moonlighting at the ballpark; Craighead had previously worked for the NBA's Minnesota Timberwolves, where life was much more refined (and more boring) than at Municipal Stadium; and Orme had to think hard to remember what his wife and young daughter looked like, he saw them so little after his life desolved into chaos at Municipal Stadium.

Bill Fisher was in charge of running the souvenir stand, but by day he was a mild-mannered computer programmer. He hated being a computer programmer, but he loved baseball, and he wanted desperately to have something to do with the Saints. He told Mike Veeck so, in the half-dozen letters he wrote Veeck before the season started. Fisher said he would do anything—sell peanuts, clean the bathrooms —just to be involved. The day before the Saints' only home exhibition game, Bill Fanning called and asked if Fisher would come in and help count shirts. He did, and before he left he had a new job, if only because there was nobody else to do it and the season was about to start.

The team's two interns, Jessica Jensen and John Spolyer, were hired with specific jobs in mind: Jessica to assist Wright with media relations, and Spolyer to help on the business end. But they were soon doing anything that needed doing, from Spolyer selling programs before every game and fetching beer and leftover hot dogs for everybody in the office after with his trademark earnestness, to Jensen working the scoreboard and selling tickets.

The result of all these people and more—friends and relatives who dropped by at will, league officials who were frequently hanging around, players who wandered through to look at the newspaper, check the statistics, or use the phone, fans coming in to buy hats and sweatshirts—added to the interminable ringing of phones, buzzing of the fax machine, and endless string of voices, some talking and some shouting, created a miraculous cacophony of sound and motion. It was crazy and often disorienting, but it was better than the dull, listless silence that would have been the alternative if nobody had showed up for the games.

Of course, people did show up, lots of them, and it caught the Saints a little off guard.

Working from that original estimate of 2,200 people a game (74,800 for the year, figuring for two rainouts), Bill Fanning came up with a first-year budget of around $650,000. That is about $200,000 a year more than the average for most minor-league teams at about that level, since the Saints, like the rest of their Northern League brethren, were not affiliated with any major-league teams. A typical minor-league club, operating under an agreement with a parent club, is not responsible for player salaries; the organization picks that up. That average minor-league team doesn't have to pay worker's compensation insurance for its players, and the big-league front office sends a tidy sum to its charge in return for the minor-league team signing the agreement. In return, of course, the parent organization is free to move players around at will—it can even move a franchise, if it really wants to—without the minor-league front office having any say in the matter. Besides being cold water in the face of a community when its star player is suddenly pulled from its midst for the September call-up to the major-league roster, it's no fun to run a team like that. As the season progressed and the six Northern League owners plied their trade the way they wanted to, Marv Goldklang's movie theater analogy rang true more and more. The owners liked doing more than just popping the popcorn and selling the tickets: they were having a great time selecting which movies to show as well. As far as the Saints were concerned, that extra $200,000 was money well spent. Plus, it was money the club knew it would have to spend. Team officials had no idea when the season started, though, that they would have to lay out as much money as they did to run the Saints.

On Opening Day, for example, fans who went out to the concession stand in the main concourse in the third inning didn't get back to their seats with their hot dogs until the seventh. The stand was built to accommodate the small crowds that usually showed up for the high school baseball and small-college football games that Municipal Stadium was normally home to. Numbers like a few hundred, or a thousand, or two thousand fans at most. So the lines at the first Saints games wound back to the end of the concourse, swinging past the restrooms and nearly out the front gate. The club had to put in auxiliary concession stands, one behind each of the two general-admission sections, plus two new beer stands, and they had to hire people to work in them. If the concession stands were inadequate, the restroom capacity was downright dismal. The team had to rent portable toilets to install under the general-admission sections for the entire season. If all those people were waiting in line to buy hot dogs, the club had to first order the hot dogs to sell them. The Saints carried Summit Beer, a local microbrew that was a favorite of the Municipal Stadium crowds, but since Summit was a small operation, the Saints' orders were stretching the brewery's production to the limit, and the taps frequently ran dry. Besides the original staff, the Saints needed to hire part-timers to answer phones, sell tickets, and handle clerical duties. The handful of vendors they originally hired to roam the stands were not nearly enough, and they had to bring on many more.

While the turnstiles kept clicking and bringing in money, the team had to keep spending money as well. By the time the year was over, the Saints had spent about double what they had anticipated, around $1.3 million—an astounding sum for a low-level minor-league club. But ticket sales were more than twice what the team had projected, souvenir sales were above estimates by a factor of seven, and when the receipts were all tallied, the team had brought in more than a million and a half bucks—an even more prodigious figure, and one that produced a healthy profit.

Not bad for a team whose chairman, Goldklang, had before the season expressed the hope that it could break even after two years.

CHAPTER ELEVEN

Is There Life After St. Paul?

On August 3 the Saints were stretching in deep left field of Wade Stadium, with a couple of Duluth Dukes shagging batting practice fly balls a few yards in front of the lines of them, there to prevent a deep line drive from thumping a St. Paul player on the top of the head while he was trying to touch his toes. Tim Blackwell, meanwhile, was looking for a Thunder Bay Whiskey Jacks roster. Why? St. Paul was not playing Thunder Bay, it was playing Duluth. He had to worry about Dana Williams and Wayne Rosenthal, not Rodney McCray and Pete Kuhl. What's going on? "Dan Schwam asked me if I would be interested in working out a deal," Blackwell explained.

The next step was to find the roster. In Duluth, this was not an easy task. The Dukes' main office was downtown, not in Wade Stadium on the north end of town. At Wade they had enough filing cabinets filled with documents, desks, phones, and other office equipment to get by, but this was not exactly a baseball archive. Often, the staff at the Duluth ballpark was lucky to have a Dukes roster, let alone one for Thunder Bay. Blackwell's best bet, then, was to call St. Paul, and have Saints PR guy Dave Wright dig up one of his own rosters and fax it to Wade Stadium. And that's what happened.

The deal Schwam was offering was relief pitcher Kevin McDonald for Saints outfielder Kent Blasingame. On the surface, it seemed like a pretty good deal for St. Paul. In the previous month, their pitching had fallen apart. The starters could not buy a lead, and the relievers could not hold one. Closer Damon Pollard, a power pitcher whose job it was to blow ninety-mile-per-hour fastballs past opposition batters in the eighth and ninth innings to save ballgames, was failing in this task more often than not. He had lost his closer's job and was working desperately to earn it back. If he could not, the Saints had no one else well-suited to take over the role. McDonald was not exactly awing hitters with his overpowering stuff, but Blackwell wasn't looking for overpowering. He was looking for effective.

Schwam had had his eye on Blasingame since the Northern League tryout camp in Los Angeles back in April, where he had first seen the outfielder. Blasingame came from baseball stock, after all. His dad, Don Blasingame, had followed an average major-league career with huge success as a player and coach in Japan, where baseball fans are demanding, but where they cherish success. Kent, an Arizonan by birth, spent most of his boyhood in Japan, bringing back to the United States a fluent knowledge of Japanese language and a keen understanding of the Japanese style of baseball: fast, aggressive, with lots of bunting and plenty of base-stealing. Had he known Blasingame spoke perfect Japanese, Schwam would say later, he would have taken Blasingame without a second thought. The Whiskey Jacks had an agreement with a Japanese team that brought them two nineteen-year-old pitchers, Yoshi Seo and Asahito Shinada. They quickly emerged as two of the finest pitchers in the league, but they still couldn't speak a word of English, and for much of the season the Whiskey Jacks had to spring for an interpreter to travel with the team so they could even have a clue what was going on. Blasingame would have solved that problem. Plus, Schwam added quickly, Kent would have played every day. Schwam was desperate for outfielders. And infielders. Any position player, really, that could boost his team's sorry batting average and would be anxious to come to the ballpark every day, something Schwam knew he didn't have nearly enough of. That enthusiasm would have complemented the league's best pitching staff, a group of hurlers that nearly went wasted for a lack of runs.

Enthusiasm was one of the things Kent Blasingame did not lack. Nor was he wanting for self-confidence. A player does not bunt on practically every other at-bat unless he has plenty of zeal and energy. Blasingame considered himself a natural base stealer who would have led the league in that category if only he got enough playing time. He was a natural center fielder who would never play there because Rick Hirtensteiner, who was the best outfielder in the Northern League and could have been the best outfielder in Triple A that year, was there for good, unless one of his legs fell off or something. Instead, Blasingame was caught in the left-field quagmire, fighting for playing time with Tommy Raffo, Keith Gogos, and a new arrival, Derrick Dietrich. Raffo, even when injured, was a perennial .300 hitter, so he won the at-bat sweepstakes. Dietrich came in second because he had a knack of getting on base nearly every time he stepped to the plate. Gogos played a little bit, in hopes that he would belt a tape-measure home run, and Blasingame got in the game once in a while so he could try to bunt himself to first base.

This was not a secret. It was not like the two typical baseball bunts: either the hitter is trying to move a runner over to second and him reaching first safely would be an added, and surprising, bonus; or once in a while the batter surprises the opposing fielders by crouching into the bunting position and dropping a ball down the baseline in hopes of a quick base hit. But with Kent Blasingame, he bunted for a hit almost more often than he didn't, and everybody knew it. After the second week of the season, practically every time Kent would come to bat, the first baseman would inch forward onto the infield grass, and the third baseman would hop halfway down the line towards home plate, barely worrying about getting his head torn off, so sure was he that Blasingame would lay one down instead of swinging away. Every once in a while he would take a full swing, and he had some success popping line drives past a drawn-in infield, but bunting was Kent's game, and he did it well. Well enough that his batting average hovered around .300 for the first month or so of the season, until the law of averages caught up with him. Even the best bunters can lay down dribblers and rely on their finesse and speed for singles every so often, then they have to fall back on their full swing and go for some legitimate singles. Kent's inability to do that cost him, and his average had sunk below .250 when the trade talk began.

Blackwell walked up to Kent in the dugout during the game, as the Saints were losing, after having gone 10-4 in June and 12-14 in July, and told him what Schwam had asked. Schwam wanted Blasingame, Blackie said, and he was inclined to make the deal if he could get a good pitcher in return, because he was desperate for better pitching, and he just didn't have a spot in the lineup where Kent could play every day, no matter how much he shuffled things. But this was not organized baseball, it was the Northern League, and Blackwell left the choice up to Kent.

This was just the latest episode in Kent Blasingame's Northern League soap opera. Like the melodramas that clog daytime TV, Blasingame's story was filled with ups and downs, plot twists and improbabilities, good guys and villains. Guess who the villain was? It was Mal Fichman, who seemed to be the scoundrel of choice in the Northern League in 1993. He was Blasingame's scourge even before the season began. Fichman had seen Blasingame at the Los Angeles tryout and was impressed with his skills, and with his baseball lineage. He told Blasingame he wanted him to be a Duluth Duke, that he would be sending a contract for $700 a month, the typical league salary for a rookie. Kent told his friends and family he was going to be a professional baseball player, and he started calling around from Arizona to find an apartment in Duluth. After he had found a place to live Fichman informed Kent, just weeks before the season started, that he had decided not to send him a contract after all. Blasingame had fallen victim to Fichman's famous trick of stockpiling players with promises and offers, then only tendering actual contracts to the cream of those who had said yes. Even during the season, Fichman invited players to come to Duluth, at their own expense, for tryouts when they had little hope of making the ballclub. Other clubs, particularly St. Paul (which benefitted from Goldklang's deep pockets) would fly players in for tryouts, put them up in a hotel, and even bring them along on road trips. If the tryout didn't work out, the teams would fly the players back home again.

After being shunned by the Dukes, Kent got lucky when there was a spot on the St. Paul roster. He signed on with the Saints and quickly endeared himself to the staff and the fans with his outgoing nature and enthusiasm. Even after the season, months after the last Kent Blasin-game sighting at Municipal Stadium, there were more pictures of him—playing with Coco, the Blackwell's dog, clowning around with Bill Murray, hamming for the camera—hanging from the walls of the Saints office than of any other Saint.

But now he had to decide whether he was ready to leave. "I really like it in St. Paul," he said, weighing his options. "The people are great, and I really like the guys on the team. I wonder if I'd play in Thunder Bay. I couldn't play less than I play here."

Within a week, trade rumors of all kinds were ricocheting through the Saints clubhouse like a bullet in a bunker. There were murmurs everywhere for every conceivable deal. Greg D'Alexander had heard that he would be part of a deal, and he started asking around to see if it was true. Everybody said no. Did that really mean no, or were they just being coy so word of any potential deal wouldn't leak out? Some reports had Hirtensteiner being traded to Thunder Bay even-up for this or that pitcher. When Bill Fanning heard about that, he laughed out loud. As general manager, Fanning had virtually no say over the baseball side of the Saints' operation, and that was just fine with him, but he knew enough about it to understand that Goldklang would sooner hire Mal Fichman as his personal assistant than trade Hirtensteiner. Besides being the most popular Saint, and the only one with a polka written in his honor, Rick was also the best center fielder in the league, with a batting average comfortably above .300 all year, no errors, and a penchant for throwing out runners at the plate who dared try to tag up and score on fly balls to center. Trade Hirtensteiner? As team PR flak Dave Wright put it, "Not a bleeping chance."

Then the latest word—and this one actually came from people within the Saints organization who knew what was going on—was that the Blasingame deal had fallen through. Kevin McDonald was the Whiskey Jacks' ace out of the bullpen, and Blackwell was offering an even trade, McDonald for Blasingame, whose batting average was dipping almost every game he played. That would not do for Thunder Bay's Dan Schwam; he thought Blackwell was not offering him enough, and he wanted another player thrown into the deal in return for his pitcher, and he had his eye on infielder Jerry DeFabbia, a scrappy defensive rookie who was hitting around .280 in his limited playing time. Blackwell only wanted to part with one player, and the impasse had all but killed the deal. But Schwam still wanted to make a trade and inject some life into his flaccid ballclub. They would talk again before the August 23 trading deadline.

Mike Mimbs was close to earning his degree at Mercer University in Macon, Georgia, but it wasn't a homework assignment that caused the pitcher to furiously work math problems in the bullpen that same August day. He had heard that Goldklang had promised the first game's gate receipts to the Saints players if St. Paul made the playoffs by wining the second-half title. Mimbs figured for twenty-two players, a manager, a trainer, and a few half shares for players who would be cut early or who had yet to arrive. Divide that into 5,069 fans, six or seven dollars each for playoff tickets, and that worked out to more than a thousand bucks a guy. That was serious money for minor-league players, whose normal playoff bonus is nothing but a few extra ballgames to play, and maybe a ring if they win the title.

"That's over a thousand dollars," Mimbs said to player after player after he had finished his calculations. "Now I have something to play for."

You weren't playing for anything before?

"Well, I wanted to do good, but this really gives me an incentive to win."

If there was anything that would legitimize the Northern League in the eyes of its principles, one thing that would serve notice that this was a place for serious baseball as much as any other minor league, it would be major-league scouts making the rounds and signing players. By August, the first part of that vision was coming true, and the second part was beginning to. A couple of Northern League players had been signed by big-league organizations—Thunder Bay third baseman Mike Barry by the Montreal Expos, Rochester outfielder Kash Beauchamp, the league's best hitter, by the Cincinnati Reds. The Saints had a couple of their players picked up before the season even began, and they counted those as signings, as tenuous as they might be.

And the scouts began to come, one or two here or there at first, but many more and in bunches as the second half of the season wore on. The Baltimore Orioles and the Kansas City Royals were the first to put the Northern League on their regular scouting rotation, and other clubs followed. Many of those that didn't send scouts to Northern League games regularly still sent representatives at least once to evaluate the league's talent, to see whether these clubs really were able to collect enough worthwhile ballplayers to make it worth the big league clubs' while to spend the time and money to check them out.

The scouts were enchanted—and not just with the baseball. These are men—many of them former ballplayers, some former coaches, but all people who have had years of association with the game—for whom baseball is such a great part of their soul that they cannot leave it. After the clock runs out on their playing days, once front offices decide they are no longer needed as coaches or managers, these scouts still need to be near the game, to take to the road to sift through literally thousands of high school, college, and pro ballplayers to find those two or three in a million who will actually weave their way through the farm system and make it to the show. It was as much a factor of luck as it was skill for these scouts; they all knew what to look for, and they all had the same radar guns and stopwatches to measure pitch speed and the time hitters took running to first base, but when the scouting report finally had to be turned in to the home office, a scout's bad day could have as much effect on a ballplayer's future as his playing ability. That, as much as anything, was why there were so many good unsigned players left for the Northern League to pick up. But to discover those few potential stars, these scouts had to see hundreds of games each year—American Legion games, high school tournaments, college games, weekend marathons of semipro ball, minor-league games in every professional ballpark in their territories. For many scouts, it got to be a lot like the shoe salesman who wakes up every morning to smell people's feet and see bratty kids pulling shoes out of order on the shelves. He hates the work, but he doesn't know anything else, so he keeps going back. Except that baseball is a game that once stimulated so much passion and devotion in these men. Now it was merely a job, and sometimes it was drudgery.

When these scouts made their way into Municipal Stadium to see the Saints, though, some of them had fun at a baseball game for the first time in years. And not just because of the game, but because of the whole atmosphere. Larry Grefer, a Chicago White Sox scout, had planned to stay only for a couple of days, but he stayed at the ballpark for an entire week. His excuse was that he wanted to see more Northern League players without having to travel to another town, but he didn't press his case too hard. After all, Grefer took great pains to ingrain himself in the fabric of St. Paul baseball. He would not leave St. Paul until the team photographer, Linda Cullen, had taken his picture posing with the mascot, Saint the Pig, and had promised to send him a copy. But that wasn't all. The Saints had commissioned St. Paul artist Andy Nelson to paint a giant, twenty-by-fifty-foot mural on the outside of the stadium, to greet fans waiting in line to get their tickets ripped. The scene was a wide-angle view of Municipal Stadium, as seen from the top of the grandstand, just to the left of the press box, looking down towards the field. Nelson was going to include everything: the host of crowd-favorite vendors like Wally the Beerman (probably the world's only beer vendor with his own TV commercial for a local liquor store, and whom the Saints had hired away from the Metrodome) and Tommy Green, whose gravelly, carrying call of, "Dooooove Baaaars! Iiiiiiiice Creeeeeeeam! Milk Chooooooooooo-colate! Lovey Doooooooooooovey!" was repeated after him as he traversed the stadium. Sister Rosalind giving a massage and the Lovely Gina trimming someone's hair. The Saints in the field. Saint the Pig bringing balls to the umpire. Grefer wanted in on it. He had a little chat with Andy Nelson. So now, in the giant Municipal Stadium mural, sitting in the stands right behind home plate, you can see White Sox scout Larry Grefer pointing his radar gun towards the pitcher's mound, looking for that next great prospect.

Usually when a scout comes to check out a game, he calls ahead and the home team reserves a seat for him right behind home plate, so he can have a good vantage point from which to take radar readings and to best see the action. (Although most scouts will tell you that if they get to the park in time for batting and infield practice, ninety percent of their work is done before the first pitch is thrown. That's where they get to see everybody swing and everybody field in ideal conditions, so they can gauge their true ability. The game is the time only to check pitching and running speed, and to eat free food.) At Saints games, though, the team did not give those seats to scouts. Not because it didn't want to, but because those tickets had long ago been sold, weeks and months before management realized either that this many people would want to come to the games, or that so many scouts would as well. So the owner's box, that improvised "luxury" suite encased in chain link and offering a field's-eye view of the action from folding chairs, was pressed into service as the scouting box as well. When the scouts—and in the last month of the season there were at least three or four at every game—needed to take a radar reading on a new pitcher, one of them would chug over about fifty feet to the five-foot-tall doorway, also protected by a chain-link gate, that in other times served as the place through which to push lawn mowers, but that now served as the pig's entry onto the playing field. The scouts had to share their space with a 150-pound porcine ballboy, and they thought it was the funniest thing they had ever done.

Carl Blando, a Kansas City scout, had been involved in baseball a long time. The first time he saw Damon Pollard throw a pitch in relief, he automatically took a second look. Pollard's pitch darted toward home plate like a pea, zipping into catcher Frank Charles' mitt for an ear-popping strike. Blando was surprised to learn that Pollard had come to the Saints via his own organization, having been cut by the Royals in spring training after three seasons of unrealized potential in Single A, including thirteen saves in 1992 at Baseball City in the Florida State League. Damon was an overpowering pitcher, but he had serious trouble keeping his pitches down in the strike zone, and he walked a lot of batters, something a closer simply cannot do. Plus, he was now twenty-five. That was old for a pitcher to be starting over. It was players like Pollard, Blando said, who make his job more difficult. Those are the ones you want to sign, the players on the cusp who might have the potential to make it someday, but for whom the organization has neither the patience nor the roster spots to move along slowly. "When you come here, you talk about how some players are on the way up and some are on the way down. It's very difficult. Sometimes you have to tell them this is as far as they're going to get."

Meanwhile, Damon Pollard struck out another batter.

CHAPTER TWELVE

Making Moves

The drive to Thunder Bay was, by Northern League standards, long. But compared to the longest bus rides of some of the other minor leagues, the seven hours (eight if Grundy was driving) were tolerable. After all, the former Salt Lake Trappers on the bus told of the twenty-four-hour treks to play Pioneer League rival Medicine Hat, deep in Canada, drives made longer by the fact that then-manager Nick Belmonte, later Northern League director of scouting, would make everybody stop at Yellowstone National Park to see Old Faithful blow, just because he liked it. Nick was a good guy, but he had a few quirks.

There were no national parks on the drive through western Ontario on the way to Thunder Bay, but the ride was a beautiful one nonetheless. Once the bus had passed the three-hour point and had made its way through Duluth and began poking into Minnesota's North Shore, the rest of the trip would be made hugging the coast of Lake Superior, with majestic pines to the left, and the powerful lake's tides washing ashore on the right. Up and down the coast, jagged rocks point out towards the water, making for an imposing and impressive sight.

Thunder Bay itself is not quite so picturesque. *Minnesota Monthly* magazine once did a travel story about Thunder Bay, and the ever-positive organ had to find something nice to say about the city of 120,000 on Lake Superior's north side. "It's true that it takes some digging to find Thunder Bay's charm," the piece said. Digging, indeed. Thunder Bay is not without its charm, but that charm is not on its surface. The people there are nice, and despite its share of poverty and run-down buildings lining the streets of the city's poorer neighborhoods—like any other city—Thunder Bay has its gems. Like the lakeside park just a block over the railroad tracks from the Prince Arthur Hotel, where the Northern League team stayed. Yet only a handful of the players ever discovered the park was there, content to limit their time in Thunder Bay to the main drag in front of the hotel, with the McDonald's and supermarket to the right, and the Subway and Chinese restaurant to the left. The city breeds that, since it is actually two cities that were fused together about 20 years before, with no downtown or single commercial center between them, creating the image of a town without direction or course.

Maybe that's why the Northern League was so nervous about the Thunder Bay Whiskey Jacks. This was a club, after all, that had sold only about five hundred season tickets before the year began, fewer than half as many as most of the other clubs. When the season began, league president Miles Wolff openly wondered about the financial futures of two clubs, Rochester and Thunder Bay. Every other team was fairly sure of breaking even, just from the encouraging signs of their advance season and single-game ticket sales. But five hundred season tickets is a shaky base for a minor-league club that needs more than two thousand folks a game to break even. Wolff need not have worried. What he didn't take into consideration was that season tickets are not a big priority for Canadian sports fans. The local minor-league hockey team, which routinely sells out its five-thousand-seat arena in this country where hockey is imbedded in the national culture, also sells only about five hundred season tickets a year. Whiskey Jacks fans barely batted an eyelash at the season ticket sales figures, because they knew. But Jacks owner Rickey May, not a relaxed soul in the best of circumstances, was downright anxious about the situation. He used to work for Wolff as general manager of the Durham Bulls (of "Bull Durham" fame) and he was a sports-marketing executive in North Carolina. Thunder Bay is not Durham, North Carolina, and it took May a long time to learn that. He began to catch on when people who would never have bought a season ticket began to show up at the ballpark on a regular basis. The difference in civic attitudes really came home to him when he had the Whiskey Jacks public-address announcer exhort fans to call their city council members and pressure them to give the Jacks favorable terms on a new lease. It was a technique that would have worked wonders in the southern United States, but it got Rickey May into a lot of trouble when the council members got mad and sounded off to the newspapers. Reporters called May in North Carolina, and he said he couldn't understand why these politicians were upset. In the United States, he said, politicians were happy to hear from their constituents.

But even May had to smile when the crowd began pouring into Thunder Bay's Port Arthur Stadium. Because they kept coming. After all 4,500 seats had been filled, they still came, and the Whiskey Jacks weren't about to turn anybody away. So when the standing-room sections past each grandstand had been filled, they started ushering fans onto the outfield warning track, until there were 6,200 of them, many two- and three-deep in fair territory—a ground-rule double if a ball should happen to carom off any of them. Later, at the last home game of the season, when the fans of Thunder Bay just couldn't let go of their team, 7,800 fans turned out, and they threatened to spill out of the warning track and onto the outfield grass.

It was, in theory at least, outfield grass. In practice, the field at Port Arthur Stadium was in sorry shape, and it didn't hold water very well. After a moderate rain, the diamond reasonably could be classified as a protected wetland, and the Nature Conservancy could have waged a convincing campaign to keep teams from playing there, lest a delicate new ecosystem be disturbed. It had rained hard the night before the Saints rolled into town on August 13, and after a day of baking sun and steamy temperatures in the nineties, the Port Arthur outfield was still like the Everglades without the alligators. The temperature itself was an oddity for

Thunder Bay, where fans had been known to bring blankets and winter coats to warm themselves through night games in July. But the heat came to the northern, usually frigid coast of Lake Superior, and with the previous night's two inches of rain evaporating into the air, the mugginess hit the players stepping off the air conditioned bus like a wall. It was like breathing mud.

But whatever the weather in western Ontario, it seemed to work for the Whiskey Jacks, an abysmal team on the road, but with a 17-3 record at home. Maybe it was being on the receiving end of the longest bus rides in the league, or maybe it was the fatigue brought on by the drudgery of currency conversion, but visiting teams just could not seem to win in Thunder Bay. That was fine, but the Jacks were 7-8 in the second half, after struggling to a third-place finish in the first half. The team still had to play half of its games on the road, and Dan Schwam was simmering with anger at what he felt was his team's unwillingness to play hard every night. He thought some of his players were mailing in their performances, and he wanted to bring in a player who could spark the rest of his team to play with more energy. Blackwell was still looking to bolster his pitching staff, so the two of them kept talking about a trade.

The next morning, after the Saints had eked out a 6-5 win thanks to a Leon Durham homer and a masterful ninth inning by Damon Pollard that solidified his reclamation of the team's closer role, Schwam met Blackwell and Jim Eppard for breakfast at the Prince Arthur's coffee shop. It was a two-hour breakfast, and the slow service was not the only part of the meeting that frustrated Blackwell. He offered practically every combination he would be willing to part with (not including Hirtensteiner, who still was not for sale at any price) as long as he got a pitcher in return, but he felt Schwam was afraid to pull the trigger. Schwam was disappointed because he thought that Blackwell was asking too much for what he was offering in return. It was two hours of cold eggs and going around in circles, and neither Schwam nor Blackwell was used to it. In organized baseball, minor-league managers have virtually no say over who winds up on their team. The farm director calls and says a new player is coming in and another has been released, and the manager has to deliver the news and live with what he gets. In the Northern League, however, the managers operate on a different level than that, having influence closer to that of major-league managers, and sometimes more. Tommy Lasorda and Cito Gaston never sat down to work a deal. Now Blackwell and Schwam were talking about one, but it wasn't going very well.

Jerry DeFabbia was observing the proceedings with interest. As the Blasingame Watch fell by the wayside, DeFabbia's name was coming up more and more consistently. Playing in the Northern League, and for Tim Blackwell, put him in a unique position: Blackwell and the Saints had a policy of asking the players if they wanted to be traded, and of acceding to the player's wishes. If a deal was struck, whether it would be completed or not would be up to him.

It was a significant dilemma for Jerry. Any conversation of more than three words immediately would give away the fact that DeFabbia grew up in the Bronx. After graduating from Fairleigh Dickinson University in New Jersey, DeFabbia spent a year teaching high school in New York City before he decided to see where his baseball talent could take him, and he signed with the Saints. His taut Bronx accent made him sound tough, but he wasn't and did not want people to think he was. DeFabbia was simply a nice person who loved to play baseball. His preferred position was shortstop, but Blackwell and Marv Goldklang had already decided that position was veteran Greg D'Alexander's to win or lose (Goldklang had drafted D'Alexander for his independent Miracle club in the Florida State League, just as with Tommy Raffo, and he was intensely loyal to his draftees), so DeFabbia had to play where he could find a spot, whether it was second base, third base, or short. And he didn't find a spot all that often, pulling in only eighty-nine at-bats while appearing in sixty percent of the Saints' games up to that point. He had a solid .281 average, though, and he was an aggressive fielder, so DeFabbia was frustrated that he did not have enough opportunities to contribute. But he liked his team. He had become close friends with many of his teammates, and he genuinely liked St. Paul and the raucous, devoted atmosphere that had developed at Municipal Stadium, both in the clubhouse and in the stands. It was a quandary for DeFabbia, but he had made his decision if the opportunity arose. "I don't want to be traded, but I want to play," he explained. "I'd even play third base, if I could play every day. It's not my position, but I could play it, and I would, just to get in there."

After that three-game series in Thunder Bay and a day off, the Whiskey Jacks made the reverse journey and arrived in St. Paul for another three-game set beginning August 17. As the Saints were preparing to take the field for batting practice, Kent Blasingame and Eric Moran were emptying the contents of their lockers into their gym bags and preparing to throw them in their cars, get their final paychecks, and head home. They had been cut.

Moran grew up in tiny Versailles, Ohio, and went to a small Ohio college, a baseball heritage that is guaranteed to escape the notice of pro scouts. Indeed, he was not discovered, and after a solid career as a pitcher at tiny Tiffin College, Moran found that no one wanted to pay him to play baseball. People did, however, want to pay him to practice accounting, which was what he received a degree in, so he did that for a year, until word of the Northern League drifted his way. Like everybody else who eventually wound up in the league, Moran decided then that it was not too late to give up his goal, so he tried out and was offered a contract by the Saints. He was used frequently by Tim Blackwell in middle relief, but often he didn't provide much. Moran was a rookie prone to rookie mistakes, like not bringing his hand over the ball during his delivery to the plate, causing him to lose control and make some absurdly high pitches, some even sailing over the catcher's outstretched mitt and hitting the backstop on a fly. But Moran had tools, like a strong curveball and a decent fastball with movement, and he knew in his heart that he could play. By the time St. Paul sent him on a plane back to Ohio, Eric was 3-1, with a 4.78 ERA in thirty-two innings of relief. He struck out fifteen, but he walked twenty-six, and that was what ultimately paved his road back home.

After he received word that he was cut, Moran didn't head straight for Versailles, though. He hung around St. Paul for a few days, as if he were unsure whether he should really leave. He seemed to think somebody might change his mind, or that some terrible error was made, so he stopped by the ballpark a few times, called friends, went out after games, and waited for somebody to tell him what to do with his future. When he broke the news to Moran, Marv Goldklang had held out the possibility that there might be room for the pitcher in Pocatello, though he couldn't promise anything, and Moran didn't really expect anything. Ultimately, he just cleaned his stuff out of his apartment and headed out of town to ponder the rest of his life in Ohio, where at least he could do it rent-free.

Blasingame had no such reticence to leave. He just split. He threw his things in the back of his Jeep and began the drive to Arizona, taking as little time as he could to say goodbye. It wasn't that he hadn't made plenty of friends on this team, or that he was rude. But his average had dipped to .203 with just two extra-base hits (both doubles) and two RBI in a measly seventy-nine at-bats. Even then, Blasingame led the team for the season with twelve stolen bases, and that was his proof that he could be a potent weapon if only Blackwell had used him more effectively—or at least more often. But Kent Blasingame had lived by the bunt, and it ultimately was the sword upon which he was impaled. If nothing else, he proved that a baseball player—even a speedy one who was a good bunter—could only get so many base hits by dribbling balls halfway down the baseline. Over time, that figure proved to be about one time out of every five, and that's not enough to keep someone on a baseball team's payroll.

But Moran and Blasingame were not released simply because they failed to meet expectations. The middle of

August was too late for that. No, they were let go to make
room for two new prospects. Marv Goldklang had struck
paydirt in the baseball player sweepatakes. His months and
years of networking paid off in a big way, when he was able
to introduce the Saints' two new players, Rey Ordonez and
Eddie Oropesa.

Ordonez and Oropesa were Cubans who had made international headlines a few weeks before by the way they
ceased to become Cubans citizens. The two twenty-one-
year-olds were stars on the Cuban national team, Ordonez
a shortstop and Oropesa a pitcher, and they were repre-
senting their country at the World University Games in
Buffalo. Months earlier, they had decided that they could
be Cuban residents no more, that the oppression and stag-
nation of their country dictated that they leave, even
though it meant leaving wives and children, mothers, fathers, brothers, and sisters behind. But they both also had
relatives in the massive Cuban neighborhoods of south
Florida, and they were determined to use those branches
of their families to conspire to win their freedom. Late one
night, when everybody else was in bed, Oropesa hopped
over a twelve-foot chain-link fence around the compound
where the Cuban team was staying. Members of his family
were waiting in a car down the road, having driven up from
Miami to whisk their newly-defected relative to safety. The
crew-cut, stocky lefthander made a mad dash to the car,
wondering whether his Cuban government chaperones
would discover him and cut his run short, forcing him to
return to Cuba for certain and severe punishment. They
did not, and Oropesa was a free man that night. The next
night, Ordonez followed, jumping into a car driven from
Florida by his own relatives. Relatives for the two contacted
a Cuban-American sports agent, who helped them apply
for political asylum and began shopping around their ser-
vices. He called Northern League director of scouting
Nick Belmonte, a Miami native who is well known in the
Cuban-American community as a friend to Cuban ballplayers. Belmonte put Oropesa and Ordonez in touch with
Goldklang, who decided that the opportunity to sign two

stars on the best amateur baseball team in the world was too sumptuous to pass up. Within days, the two were in white and black St. Paul Saints uniforms.

It was a little disorienting for the rest of the team, and for Oropesa and Ordonez, at first. The two Cubans literally did not speak one word of English. They relied for a couple of days on an interpreter who was there with them, and then on Eddie Ortega, a fellow Cuban who had left the country legally six years earlier for Venezuela before settling in Miami and beginning his baseball career. Ordonez was a masterful defensive shortstop who could also play second base—but not when Oropesa was pitching, because when Blackwell went to the mound to talk to his pitcher, he needed second baseman Ortega to head there as well, otherwise Blackwell may as well have been speaking Sanskrit for all Oropesa would have understood.

It didn't matter, though, once the two were in the game and no one had to talk to them. The rules of baseball are the same in Cuba as in the United States, and these two were outstanding prospects no matter in what country they were playing. When Rey Ordonez was at short, he swept up the rear of the infield dirt from just his side of third base all the way to the other side of second like a vacuum. When the Saints pitchers would hit ground balls to the infielders before the games, they often would try to test Ordonez's range with seemingly impossible shots to one side or the other. He not only made them, but he made them look easy with his fleet speed. So everybody knew he could field and run. But could he hit?

The thin, expressive player proved that in his first at-bat of his first game, when he lashed a double down the left-field line. In his next at-bat, he hit another double. Then another. Radio play-by-play announcer Doug McLeod was in the Municipal Stadium broadcast booth, but his shrieks could almost be heard down both baselines in the general admission seats "VIVA Rey Ordonez!" McLeod shouted over and over again. But Rey wasn't done yet. He had a single in his fourth at-bat, on his way to a 4-for-5 game, before his 2-for-4 effort the following day.

Eddie Oropesa was the kind of pitcher who drew stares when he threw. People simply watched and wondered how he made the ball do what he did. It was remarkable, but he managed to start his potent split-fingered fastball at a hitter's shoulders, and before it reached home plate, the ball would snap downward and in on right-handed hitters, making him extremely difficult to hit. In his first outing, he pitched two innings, gave up one hit, walked none, and struck out five of the seven batters he faced. These minor leaguers had never seen a ball move like that before (neither had the umpires, for that matter, and they were awfully confused about how to call Oropesa's pitches), and hitters looked foolish at what they swung at.

It was one of Tim Blackwell's great frustrations that, in his opinion, scouts often did not take the time or make the effort to really evaluate a promising player before sending their reports. That's why he was so steamed when scouts immediately began dismissing Oropesa as a poor big-league prospect because he short-armed the ball—that is, he brought his arm only part of the way back and snapped it forward instead of bringing it all the way behind him and delivering the ball in a fluid, easy motion. Too prone to injury, the scouts said. Indeed, Oropesa had a chronic blister problem on the middle finger of his pitching hand that limited him to only six innings or so per game. Baloney, Blackwell said. If a pitcher can make a ball do that, a club can work with him on his motion so it works more to its liking. You don't pass up a talent like that.

CHAPTER THIRTEEN

Love and War

WHEREAS, the Saint has dedicated his life to promoting outdoor baseball in St. Paul; and

WHEREAS, the Saint, who does all the grunt work at Municipal Stadium, performs flawlessly to countless thousands of Minnesotans; and

WHEREAS, the Saint has helped change people's perception of the porcine species and has brought dignity to hogs everywhere in the tradition of Cartoon star Porky the Pig, Green Acres TV pig Arnold Ziffel, Muppet starlet Miss Piggy, and, last but not least, Floyd of Rosedale; and

WHEREAS, the Saint has served to bring Saint Paul greater recognition, not only within Minnesota borders, but throughout the nation;

NOW, THEREFORE, I, James Scheibel, Mayor of the City of Saint Paul, do hereby proclaim Friday, August 20, 1993, to be

SAINT the PIG DAY
in the City of St. Paul.

In witness whereof I have hereunto set my hand and caused the Seal of the City of Saint Paul to be affixed this Twentieth day of August in the Year Nineteen Hundred and Ninety-Three.

James Scheibel
Mayor.

Now that calls for a celebration.

After all, as Mike Veeck remarked during the tumultuous pregame ceremony marking Saint the Pig Day in St. Paul, is this a great country or what, when a lowly pig from western Wisconsin can so enthrall a community and a game that it becomes a center of attention such that it is the recipient of international fame? And, Veeck also observed, wasn't having a pig bring baseballs to the umpires between innings a terrific idea he had?

Truly, it was. It wasn't totally original for Veeck; Jericho the Miracle Dog had already gained considerable notoriety as the ball dog of his team in Fort Myers, Florida; the dog and its owner having been rescued from a lifetime of obscurity after Veeck saw the dog delivering sacks of groceries to cars in a convenience store parking lot. Since he tried to duplicate as few of his Florida gags as possible, another trained dog was out of the question, but the animal bit goes over very well with the fans. He was just going to have to think of another kind of animal. He and general manager Bill Fanning decided to go with the midwestern farm theme, and started looking for trained pigs. Alas, they found few who were already trained to deliver baseballs periodically to home plate. But Dave Wright did run across Dennis Hauth, a River Falls, Wisconsin, farmer, who promised he could take a piglet and mold it into a top-drawer baseball draw. So they cut a deal: Saint the Pig would waddle to Municipal Stadium for Friday and Saturday home games, and for a few special occasions. Hauth and his family, in return, would receive about $2,500. When the players learned that the pig would pull down substantially more per game than they were paid, they were not happy, but that was tough, because this animal became an instant hit.

A photo of the pig was featured in *Sports Illustrated*, and he appeared prominently in *Baseball America* and in newspapers across the country. Hauth was interviewed on radio sports talk shows in Washington, D.C., New York, Los Angeles, Portland, Oregon, and elsewhere. When Al Frechtman announced Saint the Pig during the pregame festivities and Hauth took him out for a lap around home plate, the crowd invariably stood and shouted its approval. Indeed, in the beginning the pig was awfully cute, twenty-five pounds of baby bacon, waddling excitedly wherever Hauth or another member of his family would take him, pausing only to pee every now and then on the grass. When he was young, the Saint's excitement with his task was such that his handler could even let go of the leash once the umpire had collected the balls from the pig's Pig's Eye Beer saddlebags (you didn't think a stunt this popular wouldn't be sponsored, did you?), and he would run right back to his little door under the grandstand by himself. All that led to a problem, though. The pig was so popular that people began coming to the ballpark just to see it, and many of them went away disappointed if they showed up on a night when he wasn't appearing. So it wasn't long before the Saints and the Saint extended their agreement so the pig would be there for every home game, and it would only cost the team the Hauths' cost to make the hour-long trip each way to and from the ballpark every night.

Actually, the Hauths would have done it for free, though they weren't about to tell the team management that. What began for these farming entrepreneurs as a business proposition quickly escalated into serious fun. The five of them, plus the pig, would pile into the truck, bring the Saint in through the field gate (they stopped going through the office after the pig once caused the carpet to need a good cleaning), and set down their cooler packed full of drinks and snacks, and settle into their little corner under the grandstand and watch the ballgames, schmooze with whoever happened to be in the owners' box that night, and, if the Futon Living Room happened to be empty, spread out on the couch and enjoy some popcorn. Their oldest daughter, Tiffany, even brought a date every once in a while. The Hauths liked their task so much that they took it upon themselves to sew special costumes for specific promotions (like a green outfit for the team's four-months-late St. Patrick's Day celebration, for example). Dennis Hauth even rigged up a motorcycle with training wheels and a special seat for the pig, and put radio controls on it. The Saint wore a studded leather motorcycle jacket, and Frechtman started introducing him to the strains of "The Leader of the Pack," and the pig rode his hog on a lap around the bases, with Hauth following three or four steps behind, the controls in his hand.

On Saint the Pig Night, as a Soo Line locomotive stopped just beyond the left-field fence to watch the festivities and take in the first inning and a half before moving on, Florida Marlins scout Stan Zielinski sat and shook his head. In between chuckles, he said, "This is phenomenal. Unbelievable. I've never seen anything like this."

Since the first day he was associated with the St. Paul Saints, Mike Veeck's sappy side had been looking for the appropriate promotion that would symbolize love and mutual affection—the kind of relationship he wanted for his team and St. Paul—and what could be better for that than a wedding? Deciding on that was easy. Finding a couple that would be willing to participate was another matter. For some reason, most of the engaged couples the Saints approached were a little nervous about sharing their most sacred day with five thousand people they'd never met. The team sweetened the pot a bit—twenty-two sponsors kicked in the works: separate pre-wedding parties for the bride and the groom, a bridal shower, wedding rings, a wedding gown, wedding cake for five thousand guests, hair styling, the reception, and even a honeymoon. Finally, it was too good for Karen Thomforde and Ron Guilfoile to pass up. They agreed to be married August 21 at home plate.

Annie Huidekoper was frantic. Normally, her responsibility of making sure pregame programming ran smoothly could be harrowing. But this time, not only did she have to run the promotion, but she also had a wedding to plan. As the afternoon of the twenty-first wore on, Annie darted back and forth from the field to the office to the dugout, barking orders, making phone calls, and checking lists. After batting practice, the batting cage was decorated with wreaths and turned to face the stands to serve as the backdrop for the ceremony. Ramsey County Judge (and Saints season ticket-holder) Michael DeCourcy arrived to perform the ceremony. Fans began filing in and they were handed wedding programs for the "Rite Down the Middle," and a small plastic bag containing a stone: 5,068 of the bags held cubic zirconias, worth next to nothing. But one of the bags held a $2,000, half-carat diamond, and all the bearer had to do to find out if he or she was the lucky winner was to head down to the sponsoring jeweler and have it checked out.

It was a cloudless, mild, calm night as the prelude of "When a Man Loves a Woman" folded into "The Wedding March," and the ceremony began. The bride wore a simple, off-white gown, and the groom had on a brown suit and tie. Since this was a night for bucking tradition, they stood under the grandstand before the game, talking to each other, joking and laughing. The attendants wore Saints shirts (except for the tuxedo-clad pig, who was the ring bearer). The crowd watched DeCourcy conduct the ceremony and the couple melt into an emotional kiss, forgetting for that second the thousands of eyes watching their moment. Then Karen and Ron walked, hand-in-hand, through the gantlet of Saints players holding their bats skyward to form an archway, and off to their seats to watch the game.

The wedding went smoothly. The game did not. After all, the Dukes were back in town.

In the third inning, with Duluth in the field and the Saints at bat, a squirrel somehow found its way through the first-base general-admission bleachers, squeezed through the chain-link fence and onto the field. If it had it to do all over again, the squirrel would probably have thought twice about this move, but in the beginning it must have seemed like a pretty good place to be. The animal looked around it and found acres of grass and dirt, prime running-around territory. A rodent could have fun here. But then the crowd started cheering on this newest member of the Northern League, and some of the Duluth players began running after the squirrel, trying to chase it from the field. But the scared animal couldn't figure out just where it was supposed to go. Suddenly, this prospective playground turned very scary for the squirrel. Finally, it made a mad dash for the chain-link fence on the other side of the field and squirted through just to the right of the Saints dugout and headed out of sight. In the owner's box, everybody turned towards Mike Veeck, wondering what he might have had to do with the animal making its way onto the field. Veeck held his hands up innocently and kept repeating, "I didn't have anything to do with it, I swear." And White Sox scout Larry Grefer, who was *still* hanging around, shook his head. "OK. Now I can go home. I've seen everything."

Eddie Oropesa started the game for the Saints and took a no-hitter into the fifth inning after striking out two and walking one. But he developed the first of his many blisters in the fifth, and he gave up a single and two walks and was forced to leave the game, ultimately being charged with three runs and the ultimate loss. The Saints' hitters, meanwhile, were having troubles of their own against Lincoln Mikkelson, another in the seemingly endless line of average Dukes pitchers that St. Paul couldn't touch. By the eighth inning, they had managed only five hits off Mikkelson, and their only run until then came when Rey Ordonez singled to lead off the eighth and Scott Meadows followed with an RBI double.

So Meadows was on second with no outs when Leon Durham stepped up for his third plate appearance. He was 0-for-2 already; his first out came in the first inning, when he looked at two strikes—strikes being a liberal term, since the first pitch almost hit Durham, it was so far inside, and the second one crossed the plate at his ankles—and he was forced to swing at whatever came next, no matter how clearly the pitch was a ball. It was well outside, Bull missed, and he had to make the long walk to the dugout. He grounded out his second time up. Kevin Millar liked to say that Bull had two strikes against him as soon as he stepped into the batter's box. Whether the inexperienced Northern League umpires wanted the satisfaction of calling a superstar out on strikes or whether they were simply so over-matched by the task of calling professional pitching, Millar's maxim was, unfortunately, pretty close to the truth. In his third trip to the plate, Durham was determined not to let that happen again. But Mikkelson's first pitch was so clearly inside that Durham had to let it go, especially since he had to jump back out of the way. Umpire Shawn Velleck rang up a strike. Durham swung at and missed the second pitch. The third offering came and was just as inside as the first. Durham simply could not bring himself to swing at such a lousy pitch, and Velleck punched him out on strike three.

Normally, Bull took bad calls with a grim look, a shake of his head, and maybe a few words to the umpire as he headed back to the dugout. But this call was too much for him to take. So he turned around towards Velleck and told him in no uncertain terms that the pitch was inside and the umpire had made a horrible call. Durham insisted, though (and Velleck would later agree), that he never used any of the golden words that are worthy of ejection. If he had used the words "You are" in reference to Velleck and his skills, or if he had directly insulted the umpire or his family, he would have taken his medicine, showered, and paid his ejection fine. But Durham simply had his say and walked towards the dugout. Velleck followed and continued yelling at Bull, baiting him to turn around and continue the argument. Since he had been challenged, Leon obliged. The two continued jawing to each other, neither really saying much, until Velleck began to gesture and bumped his right arm against Durham's chest. Then Velleck stepped back, and in grand form, flew his thumb in a sweeping arc and shouted, "You're outta here!"

This was Leon Durham's fifteenth year of professional baseball: that meant more than 4,500 at-bats, and more than 16,000 innings in the field. In all that time, Durham had never once been ejected from a baseball game. Yet here in the Northern League, on the first night one of his children had ever seen his dad play baseball, he was tossed by an umpire who before 1993 had never called a profes-

sional baseball game in an umpire's uniform, and who had
made several strike calls that the league chief umpire Butch
Fischer, would later say were "questionable." Velleck explained to Fischer and Miles Wolff (both of whom, bad luck
for Velleck, were there at the game) that Durham had
bumped him. Both Fischer and Wolff would say they never
saw a bump, because there never was one. The next day all
Velleck could do was complain that his name was in both
the Minneapolis and St. Paul papers for being the first umpire who ever threw Leon Durham out of a ballgame in fifteen years, forgetting for the moment that his name was
there already in the box score, and any fan with a brain
could have figured out who did the deed anyway.

After Durham was done yelling and had trooped to the
clubhouse to shower, the atmosphere on the field was still
charged as Jim Eppard prepared to bat. Mikkelson made a
few tosses to catcher Gary Resetar to stay loose, but when
Eppard began to step into the box, Mikkelson threw one
more. It zipped right under Eppard's chin. Later, Eppard
would say he didn't know at first what that blur was under
his eyes, since he couldn't dream that Mikkelson would
have thrown the ball then. But he had, and Eppard began
walking towards the mound, shouting at Mikkelson with
the bat still in his hand.

When any player heads for the mound it's serious. It
was shocking that it was Jim Eppard. To say that Jim Eppard
was a mild-mannered ballplayer is like saying that Willie
Mays was a decent center fielder. Eppard was always quiet,
on the field and off, and one of the secrets of his long success as a hitter was his ability to keep his emotions in check
both when things were going well and when they weren't.
And his success was indeed impressive, even if major-league
clubs didn't want to recognize it. In twelve professional seasons, Eppard's career average was well over .300, and he
had hit above that mark eight times and had won five
league batting titles in five different leagues. He had played
for the California Angels and the Toronto Blue Jays in parts
of four seasons, hitting .281 in the big leagues. But like so

many other ballplayers, it seemed that whenever Eppard found a champion in an organization, that person would be fired and the one who took his place would not be a Jim Eppard fan. He was thirty-three, and getting close to the time when he would have to decide how long he was going to continue to play. Eppard knew he didn't want to leave the game, so he had become a Saints player-coach. It gave him a taste of helping younger players learn the game and it gave him a chance to share his formidable batting skills with others. He was always able to find something to suggest to improve a hitter's swing, and because of his accomplishments and the way he carried himself, people listened—everyone from Durham to the Saints rookies perked up when Jim Eppard offered advice. And when he made an error at the plate and swung at a bad pitch or tried to pull the ball when he should have gone to the opposite field, Eppard would simply come back to the dugout, shake his head, and tell the others in the lineup what kinds of pitches they would see so they could be ready for them.

All that does not make for someone who would head for the mound in anger. But this was an unusual situation. No one on the Saints had the feeling that Mal Fichman or Mitch Zwolensky would scold Mikkelson for his misdeed when he got back to the dugout. They'd probably pat him on the back, or so Eppard and the rest of the St. Paul players figured. And Eppard, frankly, had seen enough. He was tired of Duluth pitchers throwing at his players, he was sick of little stunts like the one Mikkelson just pulled. So off he went, with the rest of the Saints pouring out of the dugout behind him. The Dukes dutifully filed out of their dugout, and by the time someone got to Eppard and Mikkelson to restrain them—before either of them actually reached the other—there was a congregation of players and coaches on the field, just milling around, happy they didn't have to find somebody to slug. Soon order was restored, and the Saints went on with the chore of losing again to the Duluth Dukes.

CHAPTER FOURTEEN

Pray For Customers, Beg For Wins

When the St. Paul Saints said the entire second half of their home schedule was sold out in 1993, it was with an exception: Shenandoah.

If the name doesn't ring a bell, don't feel bad; a lot of people didn't know who the moderately popular country music act was, and they weren't sure why they ought to pay $12 or $15 for a ticket to see the Saints (regularly $3, $5, and $6), because of a postgame concert by Shenandoah. But when the season was young, no one had any idea how many tickets would be sold during the season, and Mike Veeck was desperate for promotion ideas that would guarantee some large crowds and revenue, he decided a big postgame concert would do the trick. Of course, by the fourth week of August the Saints needed no help from anybody to sell tickets, least of all a middling country act that only hard-core fans of the genre would appreciate. But that realization would only come after it was much to late to do anything about it.

The season's first half ended in the third week in July; the Saints' last home game was August 28. By the time the first half came to a close, there were only a handful of general admission seats for three second-half games (plus Shenandoah) left. Two days into the second half all the other nights (except Shenandoah) were sold out. It was a remarkable achievement for a baseball club, but Veeck was haunted by a specter hanging over his head wearing cowboy hats, denim jackets, and cowboy boots.

Marv Goldklang had blanched at paying a five-figure fee to this band in the first place, and the pressure was on Veeck not to lose any money on the deal. To do that, he had to come very, very close to filling the building, and as the season wore on that seemed more and more unlikely. No less than five times a day, Veeck reminded Al Frechtman in the strongest terms possible that the PA announcer should push the Shenandoah concert several times during each game, and Al did, to little effect.

It didn't help that K102, one of the proliferation of local country music radio stations and the one contracted by the Saints to help promote the event, only occasionally remembered to plug the concert on the air, and then only very casually. If a country music fan listening to K102, the top station of its type in the market, wanted to learn about the Shenandoah/Saints gig by listening to the radio, he or she had to listen very, very closely. And no amount of furious calls from Veeck or Bill Fanning to the station brass seemed to goose them into action, so it seemed the night was destined to be a very expensive flop.

Finally, though, Veeck started to get lucky. The team's popularity was so great, and the demand for tickets so overwhelming, that some fans finally decided the only way they were going to be able to see the Saints in 1993 was to shell out twelve or fifteen bucks for this one game. In the two weeks before the event, the tickets started moving out the door, slowly but steadily, until fewer than 1,000 remained on game day. Still, this was not going the way Veeck had planned. And for someone whose professional life revolved around his ability to entice people to come see the events he promoted, it was a serious drag.

About an hour before game time on Shenandoah night—a dark, gray, drizzly evening—Veeck was sitting behind Fanning's desk, leaning back in the chair and berating himself in front of Tom Whaley, Pete Orm, Dan Craighead, and Annie Huidekoper. "This was so stupid," Veeck said over and over, and no one rose to contradict him. "A streak of twenty-one sellouts in a row broken by one dumb idea."

Just then, Sister Rosalind walked by on her way to set up her massage chair in the grandstand. A slight, gray-haired woman, the sister was dressed in her usual cold-weather uniform: a scarf tied over her head, a gray coat covering her Sister Rosalind Massage Center shirt, and plain slacks. She owned one of the oldest and most successful therapeutic massage centers in the Twin Cities, and she had used her entrepreneurial spirit and sense of humor to earn her and her business tremendous exposure during the season ("Sister Rosalind and the Saints—A Heavenly Combination," went the slogan). But she was still a nun, and she never missed an opportunity to ply her craft. She told Mike that he looked distressed and asked what was wrong. He told her, and asked if she could use her connections to work a sellout through divine intervention. No problem, she replied.

With that, Sister Rosalind brought forth a sight that no one who was there would ever forget—it was too wonderful, too perfect. Would this man do anything to put people in his seats? Mike Veeck was on his knees in the general manager's office, looking skyward, with a nun looking over him, leading him in a prayer for God to send fans to the ballpark that night and save Veeck's rear end.

The sister came through, more or less. Four thousand six hundred eighty-nine paying customers showed up, though fewer than two thousand actually stayed for the concert. The Saints barely broke even that night, and Mike Veeck learned an important lesson on the mixture of baseball and country music, and of the power of prayer in a baseball stadium led by a massaging nun.

As the groggy St. Paul Saints boarded the bus at 6 a.m. on August 24 for their last of three tedious drives to Thunder Bay, they were a team for whom things were finally going right. They were 16-7, two and a half games ahead of Sioux City and Sioux Falls for the second-half title and the Northern League's second and final playoff spot. Their pitching was still spotty—brilliant one game and horrific the next—but their hitters had finally found whatever mettle they had misplaced somewhere and were now slugging the ball with regularity. No matter how many runs the St. Paul pitchers gave up, it seemed, the bats would respond with just a few more to seal a Saints victory.

They had taken control over their own destiny, but in Thunder Bay they put themselves in danger of letting it slip away.

August 24 was a day for a reunion, and even though everybody had seen Jerry DeFabbia less than a week before, he now was wearing the teal and purple of the Thunder Bay Whiskey Jacks. Through much of the pregame warmups DeFabbia stood in a huddle of Saints, talking about life in Thunder Bay (fun, but expensive) and his feelings about changing teams so late in the season (a little frustrating, but at least he was playing every day). In the end, Schwam and Blackwell were never able to come together on a trade, but Thunder Bay still wanted DeFabbia and Blackwell and Marv Goldklang still wanted to give him a chance to play, so the Saints sold DeFabbia's contract to the Whiskey Jacks for about $500, the cost of flying him to Minnesota at the beginning of the season and putting him up in a hotel until he could find an apartment.

DeFabbia hit safely in all three games of the series against his former team, and that was indicative of the way the set would go for the Saints. The vaunted St. Paul bats would fall nearly silent, and the pitching only continued to contribute to the team's woes as the Saints were swept by the Whiskey Jacks and their record dropped to 16-10. The only good news was that neither Sioux Falls nor Sioux City had managed to win a ballgame either, so the Saints were still in first place by two and a half games when the three-day Canadian massacre was over.

On the bus back to the hotel after the second game, Blackwell had a little chat with his team, getting about as outwardly aggravated as he ever got—not very much, but he spoke in clipped sentences with a clear edge in his voice, and that was enough for the players to get the message.

"Come on, we're still in first place, and we've got to stop playing like we're in last place," he said, standing at the front of the darkened, silent coach. "They've still got to catch us, believe it or not. Let's go."

The next day, before the third and final defeat, Ed Stryker sat on a folding chair beside the St. Paul dugout watching the Whiskey Jacks take infield practice. His legs were spread apart with his elbows resting on them, and his face looked glum.

"Well, it finally happened to me. My career is over," he said, watching the action in front of him. The night before, Stryker had come on in relief and had been hit hard—it was becoming something of a pattern in the season's second half, and the Saints' entire middle-relief crew seemed unable to get hitters out. His latest outing had raised his ERA to 5.40, far too high for an organization to take a serious look at a pitcher.

"I've been working since I was eight to be a baseball player, and now it's over," he continued, talking as much for therapeutic effect as to be heard. "If I didn't have a chance when my ERA was 1.9 or 2.6 with the Dodgers, I don't have much of a chance when it's five-something. I've worked hard. It's disappointing.

"I guess I'm going to make the movie, go home, and get a job," he went on, referring to the filming in the Twin Cities of "Little Big League," a baseball film which would cast Saints Stryker, Scott Meadows, and Leon Durham as Minnesota Twins, and GM Bill Fanning and Duluth pitching coach Mitch Zwolensky as Seattle Mariners coaches. "I've got a degree in finance, maybe I'll ask Marv Goldklang about jobs in Chicago. He already said I could put him down as a reference, which will help a lot. I wonder if I'd be able to do it—to stay in baseball, in the front office.

"I knew the odds were tough going in, but everyone said that if you get a chance and you make something of that chance, you would move up. I did well, I led my organization in ERA, and I was still in Single A. There was nothing else I could do."

Letting go was indeed difficult for someone whose Illinois car license plate was "ED K ER", using the scoring mark for a strikeout in place of the "Stryk" in his name. It had been a long time since Stryker had decided on his boyhood dream of becoming a professional baseball player, and had realized in high school that he might actually have the tools to make it happen.

Born and raised in the Chicago area, Stryker played baseball at Illinois State and did well enough to be signed by the Los Angeles Dodgers as a non-drafted free agent in 1990, after painfully waiting through more than fifty rounds of the major-league draft without getting a single phone call from a team telling him he was drafted. It was a tenuous opportunity for Stryker, but he seized it, determined to make the most out of it. In 1990 the Dodgers assigned Stryker to their Pioneer League team in Great Falls, where he went 2-1 with a 4.39 ERA, helping his team win the league championship with a phenomenal 48-20 record. They moved him up to Bakersfield of the California League the next year, and Stryker responded by leading the entire Dodgers organization with a 1.93 ERA, going 3-1 with six saves. That earned Stryker a bump to the Dodgers' high Single A club, Vero Beach, in the Florida State League. He finished the season with a 2.79 ERA despite a 1-3 record, with two saves. But middle relievers rarely win or save games, and their record often only changes when they take a loss. Stryker still maintains he was a strong pitcher. At one point he had the relief equivalent of a perfect game, going nine innings over several games without allowing a baserunner, and he was named the *USA Today Baseball Weekly* Minor-League Player of the Month. But he was not named the Dodgers' Minor-League Player of the Month.

That was Stryker's first tip that something was wrong with his move up the organizational ladder. The next clue came when the club called with his assignment for spring 1993. Usually, if a player has a future in an organization, he is assigned to camp at a level higher than where he will probably end up—a player destined for high Single A goes to Double A camp, for example—and certainly higher than he was the year before. But Stryker was assigned again to spring training in the Vero Beach group. He couldn't understand it, but he understood. Unless a miracle took place, his future as a Dodger was limited.

It was true. Stryker was released in spring training and was ready to give up his baseball dream then, until he got calls from Goldklang, Mal Fichman from Duluth, and Doug Simunic from Rochester, all asking him to play for their teams. He quickly determined Fichman to be a pest, and his offer was lower than the other two, so he dismissed Duluth even though Fichman called him nearly every day for a month, trying to get Stryker to change his mind. His choice was between St. Paul and Rochester, and he ultimately chose the Saints.

But now, in August, Stryker was again wondering if his baseball career was over, and most likely he was right this time.

The Northern League was a wonderful experiment that seemed to be working out famously in its first year, but there was no getting around one fact: the umpiring in the league was bad. Atrocious. The worst just about anybody had ever seen, at any level. It was the subject of newspaper articles, nearly daily screaming fits on the field from disgruntled managers and players, and boos from frustrated fans. The calls were bad in every city (unlike other leagues where crews of umps travelled from one stadium to another, the Northern League relied chiefly on local talent), and they never got better as the crews became seasoned and got more games under their belts. Part of the problem was that the league tried to rely on local umpires with no professional experience or training, and part of the problem was that league officials didn't want to go to the expense of seeking out and hiring umps with professional experience. What they got instead were people with, in almost every case, no pro experience. Only a few of the Northern League umpires had worked Division I college games, and the rest had experience only with small colleges, junior colleges, or even high school and local amateur leagues. They had never seen a backdoor slider, they didn't know how to call a split-finger fastball that broke three feet, and many of them did not have enough exposure to the rules of baseball to know even the basics of the balk rule. Many seemed intimidated by the level of play, and by the stature of the likes of Leon Durham, Pedro Guerrero, and other former major leaguers in their midst. Add to that the fact that the league had decided to go with two-ump crews instead of three, and the result was a crew of umpires who were simply over-matched.

Thunder Bay umpires were by far the worst. Because of Canadian immigration and employment laws, it was difficult to bring U.S. umpires across the border to work games in Canada. So the league figured it would be just as well to use local talent; nobody would know the difference. But everybody did know the difference. These officials were so far out of their element that they often lost control of the games, afraid to make calls, guessing and guessing wrong, and making calls regarding rules when they weren't familiar with them. On August 26, their inadequacy cost the Saints dearly.

In the top of the ninth inning, Thunder Bay was leading 2-1, and the Saints until then had barely been able to muster much offense at all. But thanks to a single, Jim Eppard was on first with no outs as Scott Meadows came to the plate. Meadows hit a slow grounder to the hole in between second and third, and the shortstop managed to cut it off, whirl, and throw to second. Eppard, who had been running with the pitch, was able to slide and stand up by the time the ball got there, but the base umpire called him out. The second baseman turned and threw to first, but Meadows had gotten there a full two steps before the ball. Unfortu-nately, the base umpire apparently forgot there might be a play at first, and he didn't turn around and look until the ball had been caught by the first baseman. But he felt qualified to make the call anyway. He put up his right fist and yelled, "Out!"

They were two of the worst calls anybody in the ballpark had ever seen, and they both occurred in the same play. Instead of runners at first and second with none out and Leon Durham coming to the plate (since both Eppard and

Meadows were clearly safe), the game was nearly over and the Whiskey Jacks were about to win. Tim Blackwell, not typically prone to animated arguing, raced out to second base and began screaming at the umpire. Meanwhile, Saints play-by-play guy Doug McLeod was in the tiny broadcast booth high above the grandstand doing some yelling of his own. "My goodness!" McLeod exclaimed, "That was easily the worst call I have ever seen. That was unbelievable. The Northern League has got to do something about its umpires!"

At the same time, one of those umpires was getting a stern lecture from Blackwell. The ump then turned and began to walk away from the manager, usually a sign that the argument was over, and the manager had best make his way back to the dugout or risk ejection. But Blackwell wasn't particularly concerned about that. He followed the umpire all the way on a diagonal line to the bullpen, jawing the whole time. The umpire didn't eject Blackwell, though, he just sat and took the abuse. Meanwhile, the entire St. Paul dugout had erupted onto the field, screaming obscenities as loud as their throats would let them, moving towards the third baseline, and ignoring the demands of the home-plate umpire to head back down the steps or risk being thrown out themselves. At first, Eppard had remained on second base, since he couldn't imagine that he had been called out. He thought Blackie was only arguing the first-base call. One of the Thunder Bay infielders had to come over and tell him he was out, at which point Eppard joined the argument himself. Order was finally restored, more or less, and Durham made the final out to seal the defeat.

At Port Arthur Stadium the umpires had to leave the games through the visitors' dugout. This was a bad idea, in hindsight. This crew barely made it through there alive. Literally. The Saints were screaming and shouting at the umpires, heaping them with insults as they dashed through the clubhouse and out into the corridor. One Saint was so mad he kicked the clubhouse door and broke it. Whiskey Jacks GM Dave True conveyed his apologies to Blackwell over the call, and said he was embarrassed that a call like that would be made at his ballpark. While milling around the bus after the game, the Whiskey Jacks players agreed with the Saints that it was the single worst call they had ever seen.

It was, thankfully for St. Paul, the last time that year they would see Canada and its umpires.

CHAPTER FIFTEEN

The Ring is the Thing

After the Thunder Bay debacle, everybody knew they had squandered their talent long enough. It was time to get serious, to bear down and win a playoff spot, and then the league championship. The message on the blackboard when the Saints arrived for practice on August 27 for their final two home games told the story: "The Ring is the Thing."

It was the team's new watchword, and it was the goal everybody was pointed towards. Forget about the thousand-dollar bonus. Forget about the notoriety and the scouts for a minute. This was a team that had come together in June with the best collection of talent in the Northern League, with a better assembly than many top Single A clubs. If this were a computer-generated baseball league, the programmer would have entered in the lifetime baseball achievements and abilities of the players on the six teams, and the Saints would have won both halves of the season by gaping margins.

But these players were human beings, some of them with more failings than most, and they had to learn to work together, to play together, to live together as a team. Baseball fans (and baseball professionals) like to focus on statistics and individual accomplishments; folks are much more likely to talk about how many home runs or how low an ERA a player has compiled in a given season or career, but they don't always mention how many championship teams that player has been on, or what types of intangible contributions he made to the effort.

But if individual talent counted for everything, every sportswriter's pompous preseason predictions would come true, and playing the games would be merely a formality. Such was the case with the Saints. Thunder Bay manager Dan Schwam made the point again and again: "With the talent Marv Goldklang has assembled, the Saints will easily win it all," he would say. "They are the class of the league, no question." Saints players said the same thing all the time. So did Tim Blackwell.

But baseball teams win only if they pull together and operate as a whole, no matter what the talent level of the individual players. That's why the Saints lost the first-half title—they spent so much time worrying about what their stats were, and fretting about how the Howe Sportsdata Bureau screwed up how many doubles they'd hit or how many walks they'd given up, that they forgot about working as a group. The results reflected this, as they grumbled and sniped their way to an anemic second-place finish. In the second half they were still in first place (mostly through the grace of the Sioux Falls Canaries, who absolutely refused to accept the gift of loss after loss St. Paul gave them; the Canaries kept losing right along with them), and the Saints still had a chance to make their season work.

Before the season started, Mike Veeck's stock line about the quality of the players lined up by the Northern League went like this: "If this league doesn't send seven or eight players to major-league organizations, then we haven't done our job." Well, by the end of August the Northern League had more than fulfilled Veeck's prediction. But except for two Saints signees picked up by big league clubs before the season began (the Saints counted those as official Northern League signings, but most observers felt that a dubious mark), St. Paul had not sold any players to major-league clubs.

That all changed August 27, when Dave Wright pulled a press release out of the copy machine. The St. Paul Saints, the statement read, have announced that they have sold the contracts of Kevin Millar, John Thoden, and Rick

Hirtensteiner to the Florida Marlins, effective at the end of the Northern League season. In the stands, Brooke Thoden was waiting to see her husband and the rest of the Saints take the field. Congratulations, someone said. For what? she asked. About John. What about John? she asked again. He was just signed by the Florida Marlins, she was told. Spouses are always the last to know about these things.

On the field, though, John didn't know either. When it came time to congratulate him, he also asked what for. Seems he knew that the Marlins were interested in signing him, but until he saw the press release, he didn't know that the deal had been made and he was back on the road to the major leagues. It had been a frustrating season for Thoden, after a frustrating season before that with the Salt Lake Trappers, following a frustrating run with the Houston Astros, trying to get the attention of his organization, trying to move up. It didn't work out that way, and he eventually wound up in St. Paul. He pitched well for the Saints, but he had a tendency to give up home runs, then he would slam lockers and scream obscenities in the clubhouse between innings. It seemed a little out of character for Thoden, normally a shy, quiet, polite player who always complimented his teammates on good plays and never forgot to say please or thank you. But his tactic of letting off steam was sometimes understandable, given the fact that he had lost at least half a dozen leads over the course of the season because of rotten relief pitching and lousy run support from his own team. If nothing else, signing a contract with the Marlins was gratifying because it meant that somebody had noticed him in spite of everything, and that he finally had another shot to prove he could compete and move up in a big-league organization.

Rick Hirtensteiner drew the same comment from just about everybody who saw him play, or who knew of his career and his ability: "He doesn't belong here." They meant he belonged in Triple A, at least, or maybe in the big leagues. Indeed, Hirtensteiner had made it to Triple A with the Ottawa Lynx, as recently as the month before he showed up in St. Paul to play center field for the Saints. But after only ten games there, with only fourteen at-bats to his credit, the Montreal Expos decided they no longer had room for Hirtensteiner, and they cut him loose. It was another level of frustration in a career that has shown enormous potential and brought tremendous disappointment.

Hirtensteiner had passed up a chance to play professional baseball right after high school, when he was drafted for the first time. Instead, he had decided to stay in his native southern California and attend Pepperdine University, a school noted for its strong baseball program. He was drafted after every season, but he turned down every offer so he could finish school. After graduation in 1989 he was drafted in the eighth round by the California Angels. The Angels sent Hirtensteiner to their Bend, Oregon, club in the short-season Northwest League. He played well, and after twenty-six games, Rick was moved up to the California League, and Palm Springs. He struggled there, as well as during the next season at Quad City in the Midwest League. He hit .224 in Palm Springs and .220 in Quad City, and that was enough for the Angels. Despite Hirtensteiner's tremendous potential, sweet swing, and natural fielding ability, California released him.

He was unable to latch on with another organization, and in 1991 he wound up in Salt Lake City, managed by the future Northern League director of scouting Nick Belmonte and owned by the future Northern League director of baseball operations Van Schley. They saw his potential, too, and at first they couldn't figure out why Hirtensteiner struggled so much at the plate and misjudged seemingly routine fly balls. They suggested he see an eye doctor. He came back the next day wearing a brand new pair of contact lenses, and he hit .356 that season.

That performance got the attention of the Montreal Expos, who signed Hirtensteiner and sent him to their Double A Eastern League club in Harrisburg, Pennsylvania. He hit .263 and made only two errors in center field in 259 chances. That earned him a move to Ottawa, of the Triple A International League. But when an organization decides there is no place for a player, there is little that player can do to change that, mostly because he no longer has a chance to play. At Triple A, Hirtensteiner rode the bench for a couple weeks, then got the call into the manager's office for the obligatory lines about how the organization had decided to make a change, and that he got caught in the numbers game. Then came the phone call from Marv Goldklang. Would he like to play in the Northern League? Rick thought about it for a while, and ultimately decided that this would be a good chance to play, to get noticed, and possibly attract the attention of another big-league organization. The phone call from the Marlins proved that to be a pretty good decision.

When Kevin Millar was a junior at Lamar University in Beaumont, Texas, in 1992, he expected a phone call on draft day. After all, he had hit .315 with thirteen home runs—second place on the school's all-time list—and he figured he had earned a shot. Plus, a Yankees scout had called Millar's college coach and asked about the third baseman, saying the Yankees were interested in drafting him. The school year was over and Millar was staying at the home of a family friend in Beaumont, waiting by the phone for the Yankees, or any other pro team, to call with draft news. No call came on that first day. No call came by the end of the draft on the second day. Later that night, the Yankees scout called and apologized. He had put Millar's name in to be drafted, but another third baseman had been taken ahead of him. Would Millar be willing to sign with the Yankees on the third day, when the draft round numbers drifted into the thirties and forties? "Yeah," Millar recalled. "I was willing to sign for peanuts. Anything, just to get the opportunity." But the opportunity never came. Even after the third day, after nearly 50 rounds of the professional draft, around 1,300 draft picks, this star of a Division I NCAA baseball program went undrafted. So Millar did the first thing that came into his head: normally a nondrinker, he rented a hotel room and downed a twelve-pack of beer.

He passed out on the bed, then tried to get on with his life the next morning.

In his senior year, Millar played well again. He pounded only five home runs, but he hit .330 and helped lead Lamar to the 1993 Sun Belt Conference championship. He thought he would be drafted for sure in 1993. After the second round a Florida Marlins scout called and asked if Millar might be willing to sign in a later round. But it was the same story as the year before; the end of the draft came without so much as a call, and Kevin Millar was left to contemplate what to do with the rest of his life. Then Marv Goldklang tried to help Millar with his quandary. He offered the in-fielder a spot on his team in St. Paul. Millar talked first with Bill Fanning, then for an hour with Tim Blackwell, before he finally decided to pack his bags and head the next day for Minnesota and the Saints. He wasn't sure at all what to expect. "I was picturing a little baseball field, with guys who just don't care, with little softball uniforms." He didn't even vacate the lease on his apartment in Beaumont, choosing instead to pay the rent there for the duration of his stay in St. Paul, however long that might be.

But when he checked into the Sunwood Inn down the street from Municipal Stadium, where the Saints put up their players up until they found apartments, the first person Millar met was fellow Saint Leon Durham. That proved to Kevin that the league was for real, and it was the beginning of a friendship and a mentorship.

Like so many rookies in professional baseball, Kevin Millar had never failed at the sport. He had always been the star. Now for the first time he was facing good pitching every night, and he was forced to play heads-up baseball, without mental errors or physical miscues. while he showed frequent flashes of brilliance, Kevin often failed these early tests. He was caught leading off too far, expecting a team-mate to successfully lay down a bunt that never came, or he would try to throw before the ball was safely in his mitt and it would trickle into left field. And when he made these mis-takes, Millar would frequently carry them with him for in-nings, letting them affect both his fielding and his hitting.

He would push too hard, and he would make even more mistakes. If it did nothing else, his summer in the Northern League taught him to grow up, to learn that bad things do happen to good people, and those people simply have to learn to deal with them. But the league did something else for him as well. It gave the Florida Marlins a chance to have another look at Millar. He was still in their computer from his senior year, when they almost drafted him, and they were impressed with his .300-plus batting average and his fielding potential. They called Goldklang and asked if Millar was available.

Millar showed up in St. Paul because a group of people were willing to pay him to play baseball, no matter how minute his salary, but he didn't expect much beyond that. He learned quickly, though, that he was getting the opportunity to play against top talent, and that if he were lucky, some scout might see him play and decide to take a chance on him. Early one afternoon in Thunder Bay, while Millar and Durham were sitting in their hotel room Goldklang phoned. "He said they'd sold my contract to the Marlins, and he just wanted to make sure that that was the team I wanted. I started crying. All I wanted was that chance. Without this league I never would have had the chance. If I go out and hit .180, I've had my chance, boom, and I'll hang my cleats up and go on with my life. I just want to see if I can do it."

The law of averages said that if the St. Paul Saints could get their collective act together, they could not go on forever without the skies opening and the runs coming. On August 27 and 28, just in time for the final two regular-season home games, the club finally figured out how to work together. For the Rochester Aces, that was bad news.

In the first game, Hirtensteiner and Eppard led off the game with walks, and Scott Meadows followed and got plunked in the wrist with a pitch. With the bases loaded and the crowd roaring, Leon Durham stepped to the plate and laced a single up the middle, scoring Hirtensteiner and Meadows. Tommy Raffo knocked in Meadows and

Durham, and St. Paul had four runs before they made an out. (It was almost dejá vú. Earlier in the season they had put ten runners across the plate in one inning against Rochester before Aces pitcher Jeff Bittiger, who as the pitching coach should have taken himself out long before then, before an out registered on the scoreboard.) In this game, they would put five across in that fashion. When the carnage was tallied that night, the St. Paul Saints headed to Gabe's to celebrate a 13-2 victory.

As the Saints coasted to victory on August 28, the stands were still full as the lopsided game entered the eighth and ninth innings. The game was a blowout, but nobody left. It was as though their feet were super-glued to their seats, refusing to get up and walk out of a game whose fate had long since been decided, and not minding that they would be trapped in the postgame traffic quagmire that followed every Saints home game (the result of trying to cram five thousand people and their cars into a stadium and a parking lot nobody ever thought would have to hold half that many). But still they were there. Nobody was leaving early on the last home game of this season.

Mike Veeck was sometimes a grandstander, but it was clear on the night of the 28th, after the Saints headed for the showers with an impressive victory and with a season-ending eight-game road trip ahead of them, that Veeck was truly sincere when he took the public-address microphone and spoke to the full house that stayed after the game to hear him speak.

He told people that even he had been skeptical of its success when the Northern League was just a concept, and Miles Wolff was looked at in the baseball world as slightly off-kilter for taking on the establishment. Of course Veeck had signed on anyway, because he wanted to show a thing or two to those major-league executives who had decided long ago that they would never hire him; still, he understood why others had viewed the venture with skepticism. Veeck reminded everyone of the disdain shown by the other professional baseball team in town—the one that plays inside the big white bubble—even though St. Paul drew ninety-eight percent of its capacity (third best in all of professional baseball) while the Twins could pull in only less than half of theirs. The monkey, Veeck told the cheering thousands, had been forcefully flung off the back of Minnesota's capital city; St. Paul had shown the will and the class and the ability to support a sports franchise—minor league or otherwise—with aplomb. "This is St. Paul's team," Veeck said into the microphone, pausing for effect. "You stuck with us, and I want to thank you for that. I love St. Paul!"

Like a tidal wave, the sellout crowd stood and cheered for a long time.

CHAPTER SIXTEEN

The Road to Rochester?

by a red-hot Mike Mimbs and the St. Paul Saints. Some of them made a tally, though, and their head count of that night's attendance never got into four figures. (It was the first time Rick Hirtensteiner actually heard "The Hirtensteiner Polka." The crowds at Municipal Stadium were so loud, the sound never made its way down to the field. But in Rochester, with fewer than a thousand folks in the house, many of them the Hirtensteiner faithful, Rick had no trouble making out the words as he stood in the batters' box. He turned towards his informal fan club, shook his head, and laughed. The catcher and the umpire just looked confused.)

Life was not so good the next night, when Rochester's announced attendance was 1,191, though the actual attendance was closer to seven hundred. The Saints were clobbered 7-1, when Don Heinkel gave up five runs on eight hits in five and two-thirds innings, and the Saints reverted to old form by leaving the bases loaded in the sixth inning.

The good news was that St. Paul finished its regular season by taking three of four from Rochester, which, despite its first-half title, played poorly enough in the second half to be tied with Mal Fichman's Duluth club for last place in the second half. Sioux Falls didn't play on the thirtieth and Sioux City was rained out, so both were three games behind the Saints with six games to play as the Saints boarded the bus to Sioux Falls. They could see the second-half crown; now they only had to keep their composure long enough to capture it.

Sioux Falls Stadium is part of a sports facility on the outskirts of what Money magazine not long ago called the most livable city in America. Most of the Saints saw only the outskirts, however, since the stadium was right across the street from the Exel Inn that was home to Northern League clubs visiting the city, and the twenty-four-hour Happy Chef that was sustenance to the players during their stay. Most Northern Leaguers never found out what was so terrific about this booming South Dakota city, but only because they never got near it.

For the most part, the ballpark was nice. The city spent a million dollars to renovate the facility for the Canaries, putting in new molded plastic seats, state-of-the-art concession stands that served far and away the best pizza in the Northern League, new team offices, and gleaming restrooms. But they apparently ran out of money before they got to the visitors' clubhouse. There wasn't one. In Sioux Falls, visiting ballplayers were forced to dress at the hotel and take the bus to the game in full uniform; they chose to do so in most cities, anyway, but in Sioux Falls they had to get dressed before they got to the park, and they couldn't shower and change at the stadium after the game. Even after checkout, the team had to hold three or four hotel rooms until after the final game of a series, when the team members smelled like they had just run around and had sweated for three hours, which they had, and they would pile into those rooms to take turns showering and changing.

On August 31, when the Saints stacked their equipment bags in the runway leading from the stadium concourse to the dugout, they were pumped up, ready to play for the second-half championship. Both Sioux Falls and Sioux City were three games behind St. Paul, but everybody knew somehow that the Explorers would fade in the final week and that the title would come down to these three games between the Saints and the Canaries. Finally, after sixty-five games worth of missed opportunities and unmet potential, the Saints had the chance to put themselves in the playoffs and prove how good they really were. All they had to do was to win two of the next three games in South Dakota.

Even though Sioux Falls had drawn more than 2,600 fans a game to its newly renovated stadium, and even though the team was in the hunt for a playoff spot in the final week of the season, and even though it was Back to School Night where kids got a free plastic lunch box filled with convenience store doughnuts sealed in plastic and kept alive by mega-doses of preservatives, the Canaries were able to entice only 2,274 people to the game that night. general manager Gary Weckwerth, who came to the Canaries via the

worlds of local television and marketing, shook his head.
He didn't know what more he could do to fill the stands.
Owner Harry Stavrenos had hired Weckworth with the idea
that he knew the market, he was familiar with the local
media, and he knew what needed to be done for the
Canaries to turn a profit. When all the receipts were
counted and the expenses tallied at the end of the season,
the ledger would show a profit, but Sioux Falls' fans were
giving up before the race was over, and this was something
even Weckworth could not control.

St. Paul opened the first inning with a run when Scott
Meadows singled and then scored on Greg D'Alexander's
infield single. They added another in the second when Rey
Ordonez beat out a grounder to shortstop and moved forward and scored on Rick Hirtensteiner's single and Jim
Eppard's double down the right-field line. Until the fourth
inning, Sioux Falls managed to keep itself in the game on
the strength of the team's first at-bat. Santy Gallone opened
the Canaries' first inning with a bunt single and scored one
batter later when Theron Todd doubled.

Then, in one swing and one very, very questionable umpire's call, Sioux Falls' back was broken.

Leon Durham was up to bat in the fifth, coming off a
walk and a single with one run scored and St. Paul leading
3-1. Heaven knows Leon had some good calls coming to
him after a season as the Northern League umpires' whipping boy, but there are bad calls and there are bad calls.
This time Leon was on the good end of a truly bad call.
With Scott Meadows on first base after another single,
Canaries pitcher Jon Jarolimek fed Durham a belt-high fastball, always a serious mistake. Bull jumped on the pitch and
sent it sailing on a line past the St. Paul bullpen and over
the "L" on the Blue Bunny Ice Cream sign in right field.
One problem, though: the Blue Bunny sign is to the right
of the foul pole, in foul territory. The ball was easily four
feet foul, but the home-plate umpire signaled it was a home
run, and the Saints were up 5-1.

Before Leon had reached home plate to receive congratulations from his teammates for his league-leading

eleventh home run and fifty-seventh RBI of the season, Sioux Falls manager Frank Verdi was at home plate, screaming at the umpire. Verdi was an old-timer who came from the traditional baseball school, and this time he harkened back to the good old days when managers' arguments with umpires were seminal events, almost as much entertainment as the games themselves. Frank stuffed his hands in his back pockets so the umpire couldn't say he was being bumped or pushed by the manager, then he went to work. With his face and body only a few inches from those of his adversary, Verdi shouted obscenities and insults at top volume, his head bobbing up and down and wagging back and forth, though Frank was careful to keep his comments within the bounds of what would keep him in the game. Finally, though, Verdi did cross the line, and the ump moved back a couple of steps, reared back, and heaved his right fist forward over his shoulder, telling Verdi he was ejected from the game.

The manager kept shouting, though. The league would fine him anyway, the call was terrible, and the fans were having a great time. Why not keep up the act for a while? But while Verdi went on, a clearly aggravated man wearing a white Canaries windbreaker and a black and yellow Sioux Falls cap walked slowly from the first-base gate just beyond the visitors' dugout, past the warning track, and onto the grass in foul territory. As he watched Frank Verdi fail to find his lost cool, this guy grew angrier and angrier himself. He walked slowly toward the field and then broke into a run. The man got into the face of the ump, screaming and yelling in the manner of the manager, throwing his cap on the ground, jumping up and down. Even Verdi was trying to restrain him. Finally, the base umpire signaled to a couple of Sioux Falls police officers, who escorted this ranting man off the field. In the stands and in the Saints dugout and bullpen, though, everybody was asking, Who was that guy? Everybody has his or her moments when they would like to storm the field and scream at the umpires, but virtually nobody does it, for fear of being arrested. But this man did. Finally, as he was being led off the field, Sioux Falls right fielder Theron Todd recognized who it was, and walked over to the St. Paul bullpen to tell the relief pitchers. "It's Harry," he said. Harry Stavrenos, the team owner.

After the fracas, the Canaries lost the stamina to compete that night. They folded and handed the Saints a 9-1 victory, allowing St. Paul fifteen hits to their eight. Saints starter Ranbir Grewal had finally found his comfortable distance and pitched six masterful innings, giving up only that one run on seven hits, and Tony Darden, Ed Stryker, and Damon Pollard combined for only one hit and no runs over the final three innings. Sioux City split a doubleheader in Thunder Bay, putting them four games back and beginning their slide into ignominy. Stavrenos left on the first plane the next morning, knowing he was in trouble. Indeed, the league fined him $1,000—a huge sum to be levied by a minor league—suspended him from his own ballpark for the rest of the season, and put him on probation for the following year.

When the Saints arrived at the Sioux Falls ballpark on the afternoon of the first of September, Tim Blackwell took a sheet out of his yellow legal pad and scribbled on it, "Magic Number: 2." That way, everybody knew (as if they didn't already) that they had to win just that game, or the one the next night, for the title, and the thousand dollars, and the fancy ring, and the champagne that would be theirs. Tim Blackwell was normally a level-headed, infinitely rational manager. But maybe the possibility of the pennant got to him; or maybe he simply misjudged the drive of his team. Either way, putting up the magic number seemed only to make his team a little more cocky, just that much more confident that eventually, in the season's final five games, they would somehow win the second-half crown.

But Sioux Falls was still in the race, and on this night they played like it. Starting pitcher Brent Farnsworth came into the game with a truly mediocre 4-4 record and an unspectacular 3.54 ERA. But in this game the Saints could not produce runs off him. St. Paul got on the board in the third inning, when Derrick Dietrich reached base on an error, moved forward on a bunt by Kevin Millar, and scored when Rey Ordonez singled. Farnsworth allowed only six other hits in eight innings, and Robert Andrakin earned a save with a perfect ninth.

In the sixth frustrating inning, Leon Durham was thrown out at second, trying to steal his fifth base of the year (not bad for a 230-pound, thirty-four-year-old guy under whom the ground rumbled when he ran). He jogged back to the dugout and saw Blackwell's magic-number sign. He ripped it off the wall, crumpled it up, and threw it in the trash. "Take this damn thing down," he said to no one in particular. "Everybody's looking up before they go up to bat. It's in our heads, man."

In keeping with the way much of the season went for him, John Thoden had pitched a superb game, going the distance and giving up two runs, only one of them earned, on seven hits. He struck out seven, but because of one of baseball's scoring injustices, Thoden was tagged with a loss. The Saints' magic number would remain at two, but the players would have to keep that statistic in their heads; there would be no sign up for the third and final game of the series.

The Saints put on their gray uniforms in their hotel rooms before heading to the ballpark at 4 p.m. on September 2, the last time they would see the Sioux Falls ballpark this season, and, they hoped, the last time they would wonder about their fate for rest of the regular season—all four games of it. Of course, the team wanted to win the second-half title for the title's sake, for the opportunity to play in the postseason, and for the championship ring, to bring a crown to a city that had embraced the club and its players far more than any of them had ever expected. Then there was the issue of Marv's playoff money. Marv Goldklang was not stingy. He had spared no expense to put his team together, often flying players to St. Paul for several days and taking them on road trips, whether they signed with the club or not. And he was anxious to pay out the thousand bucks a player he had promised his team if the Saints made the playoffs. But if there was one person affiliated with the Northern League who could, and would, try to throw a wrench into the works of St. Paul's potential playoff booty, it was Mal Fichman. Never mind that the manager of the Duluth Dukes had led his team to another pitiful half season, finishing seven games out of first place after dwelling in the cellar for the season's first half. If Mal were to see a playoff game in 1993, he would be sitting in the bleachers munching peanuts and sipping a beer. But when he caught wind of the Saints' plan to give its first playoff game's gate receipts to his team, Fichman called Miles Wolff and complained. Wolff was about as eager to hear from Fichman on this issue as he would have been to learn that Thunder Bay's stadium had fallen into Lake Superior. But Mal argued that the playoff money was technically a violation of the league's salary cap, and he claimed that Goldklang had promised it before the season began as a way to get around the limit and entice players to sign with him. That wasn't true, but Fichman was not going to let the facts get in the way of spoiling someone's fun. Finally, Wolff and league executive director Tom Leip were forced to rule that the two playoff teams would pool their respective first gates and divide them equally among the players of both teams. Considering that Rochester might bring in all of eight hundred people in for their game, this was not a good deal for St. Paul.

But the Saints couldn't even think about collecting playoff money unless they got into the playoffs. The easiest way to do that would be to leave this chilly September night with a victory.

Eddie Oropesa, who had by this time mastered the English phrase "What's up, man," took the mound to start the game for St. Paul, and his split-finger fastball was working with remarkable effectiveness. For the first six innings Oropesa pitched to two batters above the minimum, and gave up only three hits while striking out seven. The Canaries simply could not figure out how to hit Oropesa's pitches. Theron Todd, who would leave Sioux Falls after the season to take a job as a hitting instructor for the Pittsburgh

Pirates, struck out three times in a row. Most of the Canaries batters simply looked foolish standing in against the stocky Cuban. But in the seventh inning, the evil blister reappeared on Oropesa's middle finger, so after giving up a single, hitting a batter, and getting Todd to whiff on a slider, Eddie was ready to head for the showers on his one-hundredth pitch. But, of course, there were no showers for visiting players at the Sioux Falls ballpark, so instead he just sat in the dugout and let Dave Fricke attend to his finger.

The Saints, meanwhile, were not doing all that much better against a combination of Canaries pitchers Craig Lewis, Kevin Fujioka, and Vince Herring. After eight innings, they led 1-0 after Durham walked, moved to second when Derrick Dietrich was hit by a pitch, and scored on a pair of sacrifice flies from Frank Charles and Kevin Millar. It was not an awe-inspiring performance, this five-hit onslaught the powerful St. Paul Saints had wrought on the hapless Sioux Falls Canaries and their cluster of 1,967 fans there to cheer their heroes to victory. But the Saints really could hit the ball, and they remembered that fact just in time, in the top of the ninth. Dietrich opened the inning with a fly to right, and the next five Saints reached base and scored. Charles singled and scored on Greg D'Alexander's single. Millar reached on an error and came in along with D'Alexander on Rey Ordonez's single. Ordonez came home on Rick Hirtensteiner's single up the middle. Jim Eppard struck out, and Scott Meadows tripled, knocking in Hirtensteiner. Meadows trotted home when Leon Durham singled in his fifty-ninth RBI in sixty-eight games (extrapolate that to a 162-game major-league season, and that comes to 141 runs batted in). Rich Aldretti, Sioux Falls' hot-hitting designated hitter and player-coach, took the mound and gave up a single to Dietrich before retiring the eleventh batter of the inning, Charles, to hold St. Paul's lead to 7-0 with Sioux Falls getting its final opportunity in the bottom of the ninth.

Saints pitcher Jim Manfred, whose season had been an up-and-down ride of spectacular performances marred by little run support, punctuated by annoying injuries that had limited his playing time and caused him to be moved to the bullpen, relieved Oropesa with one out in the seventh inning and the bases loaded. He immediately fooled Pedro Guerrero with a slider on the inside corner for strike three, and the former big league All Star was tossed out for arguing the call. Manfred sent the Canaries down without damage in the eighth. But somewhere between the eighth and ninth innings, Manfred lost his focus, and that put the game in jeopardy for St. Paul. Mike Burton started the bottom of the ninth by staring at four straight fastballs before trotting to first base with a walk. Steve Drent followed with another walk, this one on a full count. Theron Todd also took ball four on a 3-2 count to load the bases with nobody out.

It was Manfred's second bases-loaded jam in three innings, but this one was his fault, and one stupid pitch could make it a 7-4 ballgame with the momentum swinging in the Canaries' direction. Manny stepped off the mound, took off his cap, and wiped the sweat from his forehead. The temperature had dropped into the fifties on this crisp, clear night, and it would have seemed too chilly for him to be sweating in this slight breeze. But Manfred's perspiration had nothing to do with the weather. He was about to throw some of the most important pitches of his career, and he decided to take the time to think about them carefully. The next batter was pitcher John Jarolimek. Frank Verdi was running out of substitutes, but Jarolimek had experience as a position player, and he had been known to lace balls over the wall in batting practice, so this was no idle exercise. Manfred had to be careful.

Manfred buzzed a fastball past Jarolimek for strike one. The hitter looked at another fastball for strike two. Manfred wasted a slider away, but Jarolimek was not biting and the count was one ball and two strikes. Manny threw another fastball, this one high for ball two. He stepped off the mound again and took a deep, slow breath. He stood back on the rubber, and in the jumble of signals teams use when there are runners on base who could steal their signs, catcher Frank Charles put down one finger, the signal for a fastball. Manny at once forgot about the shoulder troubles that had nearly wrecked his career. He forgot about the elbow pangs that gripped him during the last trip to Sioux Falls and put him on the disabled list. He forgot about everything except rearing back and whipping the ball over home plate with all his might.

Jarolimek swung and chopped a shot back to Manfred as the giant pitcher lunged towards home. Manny stabbed the ball and whipped it back home to Charles, who stepped on the plate and gunned the ball to first, where Eppard completed the 1-2-3 double play. That quickly—it was less than four seconds, altogether—the Canaries went from having the bases loaded and no outs to runners on second and third and two outs, only one out away from, for all intents and purposes, the end of their season. Tim Casper grounded out to second, and Jim Eppard was already jumping up and down when he caught the ball. The Saints had won the second-half title.

As soon as that final out was made, Tim Blackwell sprung into action. The stately manager of his team, the devout Christian who would never take a drink himself, grabbed the first bottle of champagne he could get his hands on. He ripped off the foil cover, tore off the wire basket holding in the plastic cork, and began shaking. Blackie then flipped the cork off with his thumbs and did a shuffle-step the length of the dugout, letting loose a stream of bubbly on everyone from Durham and Keith Gogos on one end to his twin sons Michael and Matthew on the other. That was the official sign that the celebration had begun. Fortunately for the Saints, Leon Durham was wealthy and prone to thinking ahead. He had given Trey, the team's new post-Grundy bus driver, money to buy enough champagne and beer to thoroughly soak anybody who was in South Dakota and who had anything to do with the St. Paul Saints. Added to the few bottles the team had sprung for, it was enough for plenty of champagne showers; the drinking would come later.

Everyone got into the act, the ritual bonding that comes from pouring victory champagne and beer on friends and colleagues to celebrate sporting victory. No one can quite explain it, yet no one would dare have such a triumph without it. And in the end, the mutual saturation was a lot of fun; even nine-year-olds Michael and Matthew Blackwell grabbed cans of Coors Light and sought out their dad to pour them over his head.

After a half-hour or so, when players were searching in vain for just one more can or bottle that was not empty so they could pour it over an already-drenched teammate, everybody gathered on the mound for a spontaneous group hug before the stadium groundskeepers kicked everybody out so they could turn out the lights.

As the Saints, collectively soaked in flat champagne and warm beer, piled onto the bus to return to the hotel for desperately needed showers, a giddy Tim Blackwell stood up to address his team. "The bus leaves tomorrow at twelve. The starters are whoever is standing."

It was on to a local bar for more celebration that night before heading to Sioux City the next day for three relatively meaningless games (good thing, since St. Paul was mauled in two of them), before heading the very next day to Rochester and the beginning of the first Northern League Championship Series.

CHAPTER SEVENTEEN

Money Time

The Saints ended the regular season by taking a 14-2 drubbing in Sioux City at the hands of the Explorers, hoping that all the lousy play was out of their system. They boarded the bus and began the extension of what was already the longest road trip of the year. That was OK, though; the last two road games of the year were in Rochester for games one and two of the first Northern League Championship Series. Their fatigue, it seemed, was forgotten. When they got to little Mayo Park on the afternoon of September 6, the players and coaches were pumped up. Leon Durham, for example, could scarcely hold still he was so excited. Apparently, playing much of his major-league career with the Chicago Cubs had given Durham little experience with postseason play; his only taste of it ended in defeat in the 1984 National League Championship Series, and he had never played on a title-winning club at any level in fifteen years. "Come on, man," Durham implored his teammates during the pregame warmups. "This is money time. We're gonna take this bitch. I've got a feeling."

St. Paul players lined up along the third baseline beyond the dusty infield in the chilly afternoon and played spirited games of pepper, where a hitter stands about twenty feet from a line of gloved teammates. One of them tosses a ball to the batter, who slaps ground balls and line drives back at the line, and whoever catches the ball shoots it back to the batter in rapid succession. Everybody was excited about the upcoming game and the series, but few were talking about it. Word was spreading about the condition of reserve catcher Willie Smith.

Late the night before, Smith suffered a seizure in his hotel room and had coughed up blood as terrified teammates looked on. Trainer Dave Fricke administered first aid until paramedics arrived to rush Willie to a hospital. Rochester, a city of 70,000 that is home to the world-famous Mayo Clinic, is probably the best place to fall ill if you've got to do it, but doctors were stumped as to what caused Smith's illness, even after his condition stabilized, which it did by the morning. Smith hadn't played very often; he'd appeared in a team-low twenty games and hit .220 on the year, but he had a quick sense of humor and was well-liked by the rest of the team. The players were concerned enough that they wrote his number 6 and his nickname, Butch, on the bills of their caps and on the backs of their spikes.

If there was any doubt about the level of support the St. Paul Saints received from their fans, those disbelievers were not at Mayo Park for this first playoff game. Like most sports teams, the Aces' raised the ticket prices for the postseason, so the top ticket cost seven bucks. In the world of sports, that's still a pretty good bargain—not a lot of money to watch good quality baseball no more than twenty-five rows from the field. But Rochester could only scrounge up around a thousand people in the stands, and about sixty percent of those were Saints fans. This was such a big deal to the St. Paul faithful that Saints vendors like Wally the Beerman and Tommy Green, the Dove Bar guy, made the ninety-minute drive to work the game in an alien ballpark.

Fan support is not always enough, though. The Saints played a horrible game. John Thoden, who had pitched so well all year, was wholly ineffective for four innings, giving up seven runs on nine hits. Two of those hits were convincing home runs by Mickey Pina, a late pickup by the Aces who was intended to simply fill the roster spot of slugger Kash Beauchamp, who had been sold to the Cincinnati Reds. But Pina had surprised everybody by tearing up the league in the season's final weeks, and now he leaped all over a Thoden curveball in the second and a slider in the third for deep shots over the left-field wall.

The Saints, meanwhile, spent a frustrating night at the plate. They scored one run in the first on a pair of singles by Rick Hirtensteiner and Bull Durham. They added two more in the second when Rey Ordonez doubled in Kevin Millar and Frank Charles. Then they hit a wall. The Saints went one-two-three in six of the next seven innings. When the game was over, St. Paul was on the sour end of a 7-3 decision and in a 1-0 hole for the best-of-five series. They might have been a strong team at home, but the Saints still didn't want to head home down by two games and forced to win the final three in a row, so they needed to forget their pitiful performance this night and come back the next day ready to win.

There were a handful more fans in the stands for the second playoff game in Rochester, but the percentage of Saints fans was even greater. Hundreds drove down, and three busloads came from Gabe's by the Park, the Saints' official postgame hangout.

Rochester again made the best use of its diminutive stadium, jumping on Eddie Oropesa for two runs in the first inning with Mickey Pina's third home run in two games (Oropesa would plunk Pina in the rear end his next time up, and the slugger was not a factor in the series from then on), and three more the next two innings. By the time the third frame had ended, St. Paul was down 5-2, the only bright light being Jim Eppard's two-run homer. But the Saints regained their love for the Rochester ballpark in the fourth inning. While Oropesa struggled on the mound for four innings, giving up those five runs, and Jim Manfred didn't have a much better time, letting in five more in two and two-thirds innings, the St. Paul hitters cured their amnesia and remembered how to hit again. They scored two in the fourth, thanks in part to two of Rochester's five errors. They added run another in the fifth and four more in the sixth. Two more runs came in the seventh, and in the ninth inning Greg D'Alexander ended a year of frustration at the plate and made up for his three errors in the game by hitting his first, and only, home run of the season, to give St. Paul a grand total of twelve runs on twelve hits for the night.

But Rochester still had those ten runs by the seventh inning, after former major leaguer (and probably the only Northern Leaguer who had hit a World Series home run) Curt Ford knocked in Robert Bailey with a two-out double. That was it for Manfred. So Warren Sawkiw faced Tony Darden and ripped a single into left field to Derrick Dietrich, who had replaced of Tommy Raffo. The short, stocky rookie outfielder took the grounder on the run and came up throwing as Ford rounded third and heeded manager Doug Simunic's wheelhouse arm motion to head home. Dietrich fired home, and the ball hopped once about twenty feet short of the plate and landed right in Frank Charles' outstretched mitt. The catcher had a split second to brace himself as Ford came flying in and ran into Charles full force, sending Frank rolling back ten feet. The umpire followed Charles back to the dirt behind home plate and waited, until Charles leapt to his feet and held up the ball in his mitt. Ford was out, and the Rochester rally was killed. Darden tossed two more outs to start the eighth inning, and then Damon Pollard came on and retired four batters in a row to end the game. The Saints won 12-10 to even the series at one apiece and send it back to St. Paul after a night off. It was, in effect, a best-of-three series now, but it was on the Saints' home turf.

The Saints had sold out all three playoff dates long before the series left Rochester, and the mood at Municipal Stadium on September 9 was giddy. All four local television stations had live trucks parked against the outer stadium wall, their long-necked antennae pointing skyward to beam images of the crowd and the game back to the studios. Before fans filed in, hundreds of them made sure they had had their fill at tailgate parties in the stadium parking lot—at least, those who were lucky enough to get parking spaces.

As with every St. Paul home game, the Builder's Square lot down the street was full, and cars lined both sides of Energy Park Drive for more than a mile. Some even had to park a mile and a half away at Bandana Square Mall, where the team provided free shuttle service, or at Gabe's where the ever-classy joint supplied continuous free limousine service from the bar to the park and back again.

Casey Jones, the star of a local children's television program long since cancelled, rode to the park before the game on a Burlington Northern engine in his trademark engineer's overalls and cap, to the roar of a nostalgic local crowd with a long memory. He had laid low for a long time, content to live out of the spotlight for years, but that night Casey couldn't walk five step without shaking a hand, signing an autograph, and listening to how he made that adult's childhood a happier one. But the 6:40 train that was supposed to deposit Casey Jones beside the stadium was not on time, alas. And the start of the game was pushed back even further by the slow walk to the mound of Calvin Griffith, the former owner of the Minnesota Twins, who would throw out the first pitch. Griffith was revered by Minnesota baseball fans as the last holdout from the era when baseball owners made their livings with their teams. He had finally sold out in the early 1980s to a Twin Cities banker and had retired to Florida, and the fans were now willing to forget their grumblings that Griffith let the likes of Rod Carew and Harmon Killebrew escape to other clubs, among other transgressions. Griffith represented a time in baseball history they were trying to recapture with the St. Paul Saints, and they appreciated him for that. As the frail septuagenarian creeped to the mound and delivered the ball to home plate on a roll, he received a long, loud standing ovation.

Aces manager Doug Simunic never did like playing in St. Paul, but the more he complained about it the worse it got for him. Not only would the stunts continue on the field, like the K-Man promotion he hated so much, but PA announcer Al Frechtman would eventually begin to get on Simunic's case over the loudspeaker, with the approval and encouragement of Mike Veeck and Marv Goldklang. And though Saints officials warned both managers that the game would start late, Simunic ignored the warning and did not have starter, Jeff Bittiger, warm up later, as Saints starter Don Heinkel did. Simunic would complain after the game that they were playing in a "circus," and the wait caused Bittiger to be stiff for the game.

Maybe Bittiger was a little stiff to begin with. This was, after all, the pitcher who earlier in the season gave up ten runs in one inning against the Saints without retiring a batter—every person in the order scored at least once in rapid succession. Even though Bittiger had been signed by the Kansas City Royals, with the proviso that he be loaned back to the Aces for the playoffs, this was not exactly a man who had much success against St. Paul. It should not have been a surprise, then, that he was tagged for five runs on four hits and four walks over seven innings. Bittiger got into trouble early when he opened the game by loading the bases: he walked Hirtensteiner, Eppard reached on an error on the second baseman, and Bittiger hit Scott Meadows with a pitch. Cleanup hitter Leon Durham strode to the plate with Frechtman shrieking his name and the sellout crowd cheering wildly and stomping its feet. All the attention clearly got to Bittiger, who walked Durham, forcing in a run, and then gave up RBI sacrifice flies to Tommy Raffo and Frank Charles to drop in the hole 3-0. He finished the inning having given up those runs on no hits, and although he faced seven batters in the frame, Bittiger allowed only one official at-bat according the scorebook: Kevin Millar's pop fly to shortstop to end the inning.

Heinkel's performance was precisely the opposite. The veteran mixed his pitches well, setting up his slow fastball by judicious but effective use of his slider, sidearm knuckle curve, and forkball. Heinkel would not have logged a dozen years in professional baseball without being able to perform in the big games, and all four of Heinkel's pitches were working with assurance. He was hitting corners and creating snapping movements that sent the Rochester hitters into fits. The final line on Don Heinkel: seven innings, three hits, one earned run, one walk, four strikeouts, a 5-1 victory. It was a superb performance.

Truly classy players know when to call it quits. This was the time for Heinkel. After the game he announced his retirement. He would head back to Alabama to his wife and soon-to-be five children and study to become a doctor.

The Saints entered the series' fourth game on September 10 needing only that win for the Northern League title, with Mike Mimbs taking the mound, going for his ninth win against two losses. The air in the Saints' clubhouse was electric with the thought that this might be the game that would win them the rings, and the players were walking across the concrete floor and past the orange wire-mesh lockers exuding that confidence. A local cable-television station that had been broadcasting Saints games all season was stringing up lights to capture the possible postgame celebration. Team members passed around balls, bats, and photos for their teammates to sign, making sure their entire sets of St. Paul Saints baseball cards had the proper autographs on them.

Todd Mann was sitting on the bench in the dugout soaking all this in. That Mann was wearing a Saints uniform at all was one of the incredible wrinkles the Northern League allowed. Willie Smith was still under observation in a Rochester hospital, so the league had decided to allow St. Paul to sign a catcher with the understanding that he could play only if Frank Charles were injured. Since Stephane Dionne had already left to start college in Oklahoma City, the Saints dug up Mann, a twenty-seven-year-old recreation director from rural Waseca in southern Minnesota, who played college baseball at Southern Mississippi, but whose baseball now was limited to local amateur leagues. Now Mann looked around and shook his head. "I didn't have anything to do this weekend, anyway," he said. So when Goldklang called and asked if he would like to play professional baseball for a few days, he hopped in his car and made the trip down.

In the stands, Tommy Green was hawking Dove Bars with his faithful fans echoing his calls as he walked the aisles. "This is the most fun I've ever had," he said. "I'm doing this for fun, not for money. I'll be back here every summer for the rest of my life."

After a scoreless first inning the Saints began drawing the exclamation point on the end of their season. Frank Charles had the first of his three hits and scored one of his three runs; Greg D'Alexander tried again to shake off that annoying monkey on his back that said he couldn't hit in clutch situations, and he knocked in three runs and scored twice in the first five innings. The score was 8-0 when Leon Durham came up to bat in the fifth inning. He took a Craig Bishop fastball over the right-center-field wall for that one final home run he wanted so badly to hit at home, and trotted around the bases for the team's ninth run.

At this point, though, it wasn't really the score that was important. Everybody knew innately what the final outcome would be (including GM Bill Fanning, who was busy in the clubhouse covering the wire-mesh lockers with plastic sheets to protect the players' clothes from being doused with champagne). Rather, there was a spirit present at Municipal Stadium that night that usually is not felt at baseball games. It's usually saved for religious experiences or other seminal events that are generally more important than a game. But this game represented the culmination of a process that had fused a team together, and that had brought a community closer—in short, the St. Paul Saints as an institution did far more good than anybody could ever have realistically expected. Leon Durham represented that spirit, so later, when he hit a single and was replaced by a pinch runner and he trotted into the dugout into the waiting arms of his frantic teammates, the 5,069 delirious fans kept shouting, "Bull! Bull! Bull!" Finally, the rest of the team pushed Leon back out onto the field, where he waved his cap, his massive grin belying the tough-guy image he simply couldn't keep up any longer. "I'm ready for this," Leon would say later in the clubhouse, as he was coordinating the passing out of champagne to be sprayed, and the setting aside of champagne to be drunk. "I've been waiting for this all my life. This is bigger to me than a World Series right now. This is my first championship."

By the bottom of the eighth inning, the Saints were ahead 12-0. Mimbs had pitched a sparkling six and two-thirds innings, allowing only two hits and striking out five. Jim Manfred had pitched a perfect one and one-third before giving way to Damon Pollard. The Saints had amassed seventeen hits. Then Eddie Ortega, who had been hit by a pitch that broke his left ring finger August 30 in Rochester, came in as a pinch hitter, the first time he had swung a bat in a game since then. As always, the fans went nuts when Frechtman stretched Ortega's name into a five-second scream. It was fitting, in this game of symbols, that the crowd favorite should lace a stinging RBI single up the middle, sending in the thirteenth and final St. Paul run, as Al Frechtman shrieked again, "Eddie ORTEEEEEEEEEEEEEE-EEEEEEEEEEEEEGA!"

The time was near. This was one of the most lopsided blowouts any baseball fan would ever watch: thirteen runs, eighteen hits, no errors, versus no runs, two hits, five errors. But not one member of the sellout crowd had left. There was important business yet to attend to.

Damon Pollard was on the mound facing Steve Dailey with two outs in the top of the ninth. Pollard was so pumped up that there is no telling what a radar gun would have registered had someone thought to bring one. He reared back and fired a fastball into Frank Charles' mitt for strike one. Dailey swung at another fastball he never saw for strike two. There was no mystery here. Dailey knew the next pitch would be heat, but it wasn't a fair fight. He swung and missed, and almost as part of his pitching motion, Pollard leaped into the air twice, his arms outstretched, and ran towards home plate and into the arms of Frank Charles.

On cue, Saints players ran out onto the field, shaking their champagne bottles in the direction of the small mob of players who were already in a knot around the pitcher's mound. Veeck and Goldklang pushed open the gates of the owners' box and threw themselves into the middle of the eruption, hugging anyone they found wearing a white polyester uniform. Fans streamed in like flowing ribbons from the stairs beside the dugouts, rushing onto the field to add their own hugs to the celebration. Soon, more than a thousand people were on the field, screaming wildly and hugging everybody and everything in sight.

Mike Veeck moved off to an empty area by himself and began to cry. All season long he had tried to convince people that while it was nice being Bill Veeck's son, it was a birthright he didn't need; that this was his team and this would be his legacy. But his tears belied that sentiment, and as he finally, totally let his emotions pour out, he looked up. "I just wish Dad could have been here to see this," he said, simply. "He would have liked this."

Slowly, carefully, the Saints made their way back to the dugout, where they passed a gantlet of St. Paul police officers keeping the fans on the other side of the dugout fence. In the clubhouse, nobody rested until he had hugged everybody else in the room and had poured champagne or beer on almost as many people. Rey Ordonez was being interviewed live on television, reciting over and over his newest English prase: "Only champions!"

Outside the clubhouse, the fans had not left. There were now more than 1,500 of them, pushing against the dugout fence, held back by the cadre of St. Paul cops. They were doing plenty of hugging and high-fiving themselves, and they began a chant. "We want Bull! We want Bull!" So once again, Leon Durham, this time clad only in his uniform pants and a soaked T-shirt, walked from the clubhouse into the dugout with a bottle of champagne, shaking it, and he sprayed it on the horde of fans who were pressed against the dugout fence and just wouldn't leave. People opened their mouths to take in the victory bubbly as Durham made his way down the bench.

Finally, after all the champagne and beer was gone and there was nothing left to pour on anybody, after the TV crew had packed up and gone home, after the throng finally started thinning out beyond the clubhouse door, the Saints began showering and prepared to head over to Gabe's, where the bar was putting on a party for the team that had meant so much to its business in the preceding three months. In the bar's back room, players, friends, and family piled in for free drinks and a buffet, and for more hugging. Instead of the usual crew behind the bar, though, it was Tim Blackwell, Mike Veeck, Marv Goldklang, and Bill Fanning. For a while, they handled bartending duties (and most likely no one will ever again see Tim Blackwell pouring drinks for anyone). Then, they called for quiet and got it, more or less.

It was time for the presentations. One by one, Blackie said a few words about each player and had him come to the bar to collect his championship T-shirt, and a thousand-dollar check (to hell with the league, as far as Goldklang was concerned. If he wanted to reward his team for a special year, he could reach into his pocket and do it), and to be measured for his championship ring.

Long after 1:00 a.m., when the law says Gabe's should have been closed, the Saints stayed in the back room, hugging even more and talking. Tommy Raffo put it well when he described the Northern League as not major-league, but not minor-league either. It was a new entity, totally different than anything else anybody had come up with before.

But few of those players would be back next year. Most of them were trying to wriggle their way back into that oppressive major-league farm system; as suffocating as it was, it was still the realization of the dream. One by one, they packed up their cars or headed for the airport, trying to make the next step of their dream real.

The following day, in the fog of the morning after such a frenetic celebration, the Saints office staff was back at work trying to pick up the pieces, to sort out what had happened the night and the season before from the business standpoint. Jim Eppard came in to see Marv Goldklang and to shake his hand.

Eppard said he wanted to thank Goldklang for a special season, and to officially announce his retirement as an active player, choosing to pursue his dream of coaching full-time. But, he said, he couldn't think of a better place to have spent his final season between the lines.

For Eppard, and for the Saints, it was a fitting way to end.

EPILOGUE

After learning the lessons of success in 1993, the Northern League and the St. Paul Saints spent the winter preparing for the 1994 season. One of the first things the league did was to disband the Rochester Aces franchise and award that team's slot to a new entry from Winnipeg, the Gold Eyes. Far from the apathy the Rochester area often showed for its club, the residents of Winnipeg could not wait for baseball to start. The club held a contest to name the team and received thousands of entries. The team office could barely keep up with would-be ticket buyers, waiting to get their seats for Winnipeg's 22,000-seat stadium, which was also home to the city's Canadian Football League franchise. The club's ownership group included some part-owners of the Winnipeg Jets of the National Hockey League.

Meeting in October, the league's owners voted to postpone expansion, with the understanding that they would consider growing the Northern League to at least eight teams if 1994 saw success similar to that of the inaugural season. Duluth owner Bruce Engel, whose grand visions of the Northern League becoming the building block for a third major league did not match those of his colleagues, sold his franchise and began plans to start another independent league in his native Pacific northwest. He would be able to hire Mal Fichman again, though; the Dukes' new owner fired the manager. Thunder Bay manager Dan Schwam was hired to return in 1994, as was Sioux City skipper Ed Nottle. Rochester manager Doug Simunic got his old job back, in a manner of speaking, earning the post in Winnipeg. In the middle of February Sioux Falls was still trying to settle its managerial situation. Rich Aldretti, who in 1993 was the player-coach for the Canaries, was a shoe-in for the job, but just before he was supposed to leave South Dakota for the season he was busted for possessing a small amount of marijuana and was released by the club.

Before the 1993 season started, Northern League officials were expressing the hope that as many as ten of their players would have their contracts purchased by big league organizations—that, they said, would be the sign that the league was a success in baseball terms. By the time the twenty-eight major league clubs opened their spring training camps in late February, sixteen organizations had purchased the contracts of three dozen Northern League players and coaches, and dozens more had received non-roster invitations to training camps with the opportunity to make teams' minor league rosters.

As for the Saints, the winter of 1993-94 was a busy one. The first priority—before anyone even thought about what the team would look like on the field—was to make sure there were enough seats and parking places to accommodate everybody. A 1993 Saints seat was the hottest ticket in town, and the team wanted to cash in on the interest that was still swirling around the Twin Cities' only outdoor professional baseball stadium. After a winter of negotiations with the city of St. Paul and its new mayor, Norm Coleman, Saints executives were hopeful by the middle of February that their new lease would include provisions for the city to build between 1,200 and 2,000 new seats, and to construct a tunnel under the railroad tracks beyond left field so fans could park in the large empty lot on the other side.

The club expanded its season ticket base to at least 1,600—more if the new seats were built—but it was still left with a waiting list of more than 1,000 names, since more than ninety percent of the 1993 season ticket-holders had renewed their orders.

On the field, Tim Blackwell's mustache would be back in the dugout in 1994, and he would be spending some time in the front office as well. Blackwell said he would have considered a Double A or Triple A managerial job or a major league coaching position, but the only offer that came his way after the Winter Meetings was a Triple A coaching job. That wasn't enough to overcome the independent baseball bug that had infected Blackwell and his family, and they made plans to return to St. Paul with Tim as manager, with the added responsibility of being in charge of player personnel matters.

Player-coach Jim Eppard had come to the Saints to learn how to coach after a dozen years as a player, and he did just that. Sioux Falls was interested in hiring Eppard as its manager, but he opted for having more room for advancement (and for being closer to his southern California home), taking a job as a coach with Central Valley, the Colorado Rockies' advanced Single A team in the California League.

Immediately after the season ended, Leon Durham, along with Scott Meadows, Ed Stryker, general manager Bill Fanning, and Duluth pitching coach Mitch Zwolensky landed roles in the feature film "Little Big League," which was filming at the Metrodome. Everybody had bit parts worth $100 a day except for Durham, whose role as an aging slugger called for lines, and he was paid $5,000 a week for his efforts.

The Saints offered Eppard's player-coach job to Leon Durham, since Durham found he enjoyed his unofficial coaching role in 1993 more than he thought he would. After his agent wasn't able to scare up interest from any major league organizations, Durham headed to Mexico in February to play and polish his skills until it was time to head for Minnesota and his new coaching career.

It turned out that the St. Paul Saints were as much a part of Eddie Ortega's life as he was of its. When Ortega fell in love over the winter in Mexico and planned an April wedding, he called the Saints office and said it would mean a lot if someone from the club could be there. The Saints, in return, asked him back for another year.

Frank Charles, after performing so poorly in the first part of the season, wound up playing impressively enough that he signed a contract with the Texas Rangers for their Double A club in Tulsa, Oklahoma.

Rick Hirtensteiner, one of the three Saints whose contracts were purchased by the Florida Marlins, was the only one of the trio the Marlins sent to play winter ball in Australia. Hirtensteiner hit .303 for the Melbourne Monarchs in one hundred nine at-bats before breaking his hand and heading home for surgery. He was expected to be in shape in time for the opening of spring training.

Kevin Millar went home to California for the winter to work out and prepare to report to Double A camp for the Marlins, expecting to be assigned either to the Double A club in Portland, Maine, or to the Single A clubs in Brevard County, Florida, or Kane County, Illinois.

John Thoden was in much the same situation, though his previous minor league experience made it much more likely that he would begin the season in Portland.

Ranbir Grewal was unable to snare an invitation to spring training with any major league organization, and in the middle of February it looked like he would be back with the Saints in 1994.

After keeping his batting average above .300 virtually all season, Scott Meadows earned an invitation to camp with the Rangers, with the opportunity to make the Triple A club in Oklahoma City.

Damon Pollard's fastball and his late-season discovery of the strike zone were enough for the Milwaukee Brewers, an organization in desperate search for a closer. They signed Pollard to be their closer at Double A El Paso in the Texas League.

The famous Cubans, Rey Ordonez and Eddie Oropesa, were in such demand that Major League Baseball held a lottery to assign the rights to the two players. The Mets won the rights to Ordonez and signed the speedy shortstop to a contract with a signing bonus reported to be between

$75,000 and $125,000. Ordonez might have caught a break by signing with the worst team in baseball; assuming Ordonez proved very quickly he can hit, the club planned to move him immediately to Triple A and send him to the majors as soon as he showed he was ready. In February Oropesa was still negotiating with the Cincinnati Reds, who owned his rights, but he was expected to sign in time for the start of training camp.

Jim Manfred thought his career was over, and he was prepared to settle down with his new wife and daughter and work at this landscaping business. But the Colorado Rockies ended that notion, signing Manfred to a Double A contract.

The Saints planned to invite Tony Darden to spring training in May, with the opportunity to win his spot on the club again.

Willie Smith returned home to Sacramento to recover from his illness. He informed the Saints he would like to return, and the team said it would give Smith a chance to win the catching spot in spring training.

The Saints exercised their option on Greg D'Alexander, and they planned in the spring to decide whether he would be the team's starting third baseman or if they would trade him to a club where he could play every day.

Michael Mimbs got rid of his Hollywood agent, and his new one landed him a Double A contract with the Montreal Expos.

Stephane Dionne was playing regularly and attending classes at Oklahoma City University. He made the Dean's List his first semester.

Edson Hoffman, signed late in the 1993 season, only made three appearances and pitched well in two of them (the third outing exploded his earned run average to an unrepresentative double-digit figure). The Saints offered him a contract to return in 1994 and Edson accepted, he said, "In a heartbeat."

Derrick Dietrich, also signed at the tail end of the 1993 season, proved he could both hit in the clutch and come through in the field. The Saints asked Dietrich back as well, and he accepted.

Ed Stryker got an agent after the season ended, but without any real expectation of ever playing professional baseball again. With Marv Goldklang listed as a reference on his resumé, Stryker set out to get a job in finance.

Keith Gogos played well in his native Australia over the winter, hitting over .300 with five home runs for the Melbourne Monarchs. He realized his future in American baseball was dim, so he was considering taking an offer to play professional baseball in Taiwan—for more than ten times his Northern League salary.

Eric Moran spent much of the winter working at Bucky Dent's baseball school in Florida, and was hoping to earn an invitation to training camp with somebody. Failing that, he planned to attend the March Northern League tryout camp in Florida.

Jerry DeFabbia was released by Thunder Bay, and he really wanted to come back with the Saints. St. Paul was ambivalent about that possibility, so DeFabbia's future was uncertain as he prepared to head for the March tryout camp.

Kent Blasingame was invited to camp with the Philadelphia Phillies, where his dad was in charge of the Phillies' minor league system.

Abraham Elliot Heinkel was born December 29, 1993, the fifth child of Don and Angela Heinkel. Don was attending classes at the University of Alabama-Birmingham, preparing to take his MCAT exams and head back to medical school.

Tommy Raffo waited for an invitation to spring training that never came, then accepted an offer to be an assistant baseball coach at Mississippi State University, his alma mater. But he and his wife Paula were still deciding whether to give that up and return to St. Paul to play for the Saints one more year.